Organisations and Humanisation

Every now and then when there is a discussion about problematic situations in organisations someone will talk about making organisations more 'humane'. Who, if asked, would disagree that organisations should be humane and humanisation is important? Of course, the trouble only begins when we need to explain what this means.

Organisation studies are concerned with understanding organisation and their role in society. Often new perspectives and methods are developed for improvement. There is a tendency to produce universal blueprints. Such theory is, just like management practice, always somehow grounded in assumptions about being human; about individuality and sociality, power, self-realisation and creativity, motivation, ethics, etc. One look at 'airport literature' will easily make this list longer. Most of all, management is based on ideas of what makes sense and what is worth doing.

In this book a variety of authors reflect on their experiences to discuss what it means to them to 'humanise'. What did humanisation mean to a CEO of a forensic psychiatric clinic, to a health administrator, to a teacher, to a young consultant? The contributions vary on two seemingly opposed philosophical anthropologies. What is the universal human nature or essence that organisations can and should reflect? Or should we rather organise according to intuitions, to sense that cannot be expressed?

This book then does not offer clear-cut strategies and roadmaps. It invites the reader to reflect on what it is to be human in organisations and from this perspective to reconsider practices and ideals, interventions and challenges.

Myrte van de Klundert is completing her MA in philosophy at Erasmus University Rotterdam, the Netherlands, and is Chief Editor of *Partage Student Journal*.

Robert van Boeschoten is a Lecturer and Researcher at the University of Humanistic Studies in Utrecht and the University for Applied Sciences in Amsterdam, the Netherlands.

Organisations and Humanisation

Perspectives on organising humanisation
and humanising organisations

Edited by
Myrte van de Klundert
and Robert van Boeschoten

LONDON AND NEW YORK

First published 2017
by Routledge
2 Park Square, Milton Park, Abingdon, Oxon OX14 4RN

and by Routledge
711 Third Avenue, New York, NY 10017

Routledge is an imprint of the Taylor & Francis Group, an informa business

© 2017 selection and editorial material, Myrte van de Klundert and Robert van Boeschoten; individual chapters, the contributors

The right of the editors to be identified as the authors of the editorial material, and of the authors for their individual chapters, has been asserted in accordance with sections 77 and 78 of the Copyright, Designs and Patents Act 1988.

All rights reserved. No part of this book may be reprinted or reproduced or utilised in any form or by any electronic, mechanical, or other means, now known or hereafter invented, including photocopying and recording, or in any information storage or retrieval system, without permission in writing from the publishers.

Every effort has been made to contact copyright holders for their permission to reprint material in this book. The publishers would be grateful to hear from any copyright holder who is not here acknowledged and will undertake to rectify any errors or omissions in future editions of this book.

Trademark notice: Product or corporate names may be trademarks or registered trademarks, and are used only for identification and explanation without intent to infringe.

British Library Cataloguing in Publication Data
A catalogue record for this book is available from the British Library

Library of Congress Cataloging in Publication Data
A catalog record for this book has been requested

ISBN: 978-1-4724-6821-5 (hbk)
ISBN: 978-1-315-59907-6 (ebk)

Contents

List of contributors vii
Foreword by Stephen Linstead xi
Preface xxi
Acknowledgements xxix

1 **The process of humanisation** 1
FERNANDO SUÁREZ-MÜLLER

2 **Let's dance: on humanising and organisations** 11
RUUD KAULINGFREKS

3 **A sense of consultancy: the humanising effort of problematisation** 20
MARTIJN SIMONS

4 **Humanisation, technology and organisation** 30
MYRTE VAN DE KLUNDERT AND ROBERT VAN BOESCHOTEN

5 **The humanisation of education: teaching the wisdom of uncertainty** 41
MARTIEN SCHREURS

6 **Leadership and humanisation in a forensic psychiatric clinic** 50
GABRIËL ANTHONIO AND MYRTE VAN DE KLUNDERT

7 **Humanisation in the advertising industry** 61
VERONICA MILLAN CACERES

8 **Discourse and humanisation in health care organisations** 71
CLÓVIS RICARDO MONTENEGRO DE LIMA

9 **Humanisation of the economy** 79
CHRISTIAN FELBER AND FERNANDO SUÁREZ-MÜLLER

Index 88

Contributors

Gabriël Anthonio (1963)
After studying social work and education Anthonio completed his PhD in 2006 on *Humanization of a Judicial Organization* at the University of Humanistic Studies in Utrecht. Anthonio has worked for more than thirty years in the healthcare industry including over twenty years as manager/director. In addition to his managing work, he is a professor at Stenden University in Leeuwarden. His chair is in the field of leadership and change management. Anthonio is focused on people-oriented and value-driven leadership and meaningful changes in organisations.

Robert van Boeschoten (1957)
Van Boeschoten studied social work and philosophy at the University of Amsterdam, where he then completed his PhD on philosophy and media culture (1998). Since 2004 he has been a lecturer/researcher at the University of Humanistic Studies in Utrecht and the University for Applied Sciences in Amsterdam (HvA, media department). He was the coordinator (2004–2012) of the part-time PhD program of the UvH, interim manager of the media lab of the HvA and a consultant for online startups (2000–2006). His main interest is in culture and technology and organisation studies.

Christian Felber (1972)
Felber received his masters degree in philosophy in 1996. He has taught since 2009 at Vienna University of Economics and Business, University of Graz, University of Klagenfurt and the Polytechnic University of Valencia. Since 1998 he has published fourteen books on the economy and other topics like money and ecology. Among the publications were: *Geld. Die neuen Spielregeln* (2014), *Economy for the common good* (2014) and *Let's save the euro* (2012) (all with Deuticke publishers). He has received various awards for his work, amongst which are the Premio Nueva Civilización (University of Chili 2014) and Teaching Prize (University of Graz 2013). His interests are in the development of Economy for the Common Good.

Ruud Kaulingfreks (1953)
Kaulingfreks studied sociology and philosophy at Santiago de Chile, Tiburg and Amsterdam. After working for 15 years in art schools he moved to organisation studies and became a management consultant. Currently he combines his consultancy work with academic work at the University for Humanistics at Utrecht. He is honorary professor and a member of the Centre for Philosophy and Political Economy at the Management Centre of the University of Leicester. Since he has not forgotten about his aesthetic passions, in his

research he combines philosophy, art and organisation theory. He lives in Rotterdam and would like to travel and climb mountains much more than he does now.

Myrte van de Klundert (1989)
Van de Klundert received her bachelor's degree in 2013 from the University for Humanistic Studies (cum laude). She has worked as a teaching assistant and held a few managing positions in student representation, student organisations and as a volunteer at conferences. She is currently chief editor of *Partage Student Journal*. She is now finishing her MA in philosophy at Erasmus University Rotterdam. Her interests concern gender, time, health, education, technology, identity, sense making and spirituality. She has published about egg vitrification, home birth and education. She is in training as a zen teacher (because of course, you need to stop thinking sometimes).

Clóvis Ricardo Montenegro de Lima (1960)
De Lima received his masters degree in Information Science from Universidade Federal do Rio de Janeiro (1992) and in Administração Hospitalar e de Sistemas de Saúde from Fundação Getulio Vargas – SP (1993). After that he completed two doctorate studies, one in Administration from Fundação Getulio Vargas – SP (2000) and one in Information Science from Universidade Federal do Rio de Janeiro (2005). He was the coordinator of Working Group 5 – Politics and Economics of Information ANCIB (National Association of Research and Graduate Studies in Information Science) from 2011 to 2014. Momentarily he is the editor of the journals *Logeion – Philosophy of Information* and *P2P & Innovation* and teaches at the Institute of Business and Information Technology where his research interests are focussed on the theory of communicative action and discourse, learning and innovation, intellectual freedom, regulation, management of complex organisations and ethics in organisations.

Stephen Linstead (1952)
Linstead is professor of Critical Management at York University. He has held Chairs in Wollongong (New South Wales), Sunderland, Essex and Durham and was a Visiting Scholar at Hong Kong University of Science and Technology. He studied English literature in Keele and Leeds. He has a masters in organisation development and a PhD from Sheffield Hallam University. As an author he has written many books and articles about organisational theory with special interests in philosophy, aesthetics, language, gender and sexuality, qualitative methods, ethnography and culture. He is currently developing interests in aspects of globalisation and postcolonialism; the ontology and practice of play especially in organisational and social intervention; and the use of music and song as a form of ethnographic representation.

Veronica Millan Caceres (1976)
After receiving her MBA at the Rotterdam Erasmus University, Millan Caceres completed her PhD at the University of Humanistic Studies in Utrecht on the advertising industry in times of liquidity. Her work has been centred on project management in the marketing and advertising industry. She currently is the regional IT director of a major advertising company. Her interests are in technology strategies for human interaction that incorporate the changes in the advertising industry along with the rapid evolution in technology.

Martien Schreurs (1966)
In 2003 Schreurs received his doctorate at the University of Humanistic Studies for his work on 'Bildung' in contemporary literature. Since 2005 he has been an enthusiastic

lecturer at this University. During multiple periods he also taught in various secondary schools. He organises many provocative debates and talks on 'Bildung' and education in general in and outside of the university and his research topics include humanism, nihilism, literature and Bildung.

Martijn Simons (1985)
Simons graduated with a degree in Humanistic Studies at the University of Humanistic Studies in Utrecht and in Philosophy at the University of Amsterdam. He has worked as a teaching assistant in many courses. He specialises in critical organisation and intervention studies and wrote his thesis on a Bergsonian conception of vital knowledge creation in organisations. Currently he is owner of Martijn Simons *ART* (Advies, Research and Training) and works freelance for *Kickstart your Social Impact*.

Fernando Suárez-Müller (1964)
After receiving his doctorate from the departments of philosophy and literature at the University of Amsterdam Suárez-Müller became an assistant professor of ethics and social philosophy, especially of environmental philosophy and critical organisation theory, at the University of Humanistic Studies (2010) in Utrecht (the Netherlands). He publishes in different languages (Dutch, English, German, Spanish) on a variety on philosophical topics (Foucault, Derrida, Kant). His main interests are in ethics, sustainability and economics.

Foreword
Being human

Stephen Linstead

> I'm only human,
> Of flesh and blood I'm made.
> I'm only human,
> Born to make mistakes.[1]

Being human is often associated with frailty, and mortality. Organisations, as Burkard Sievers has eloquently set out, can be seen as a defence against mortality, and indeed, a bid for immortality by those who control them. They change, but remain. They are not the same, but outlast by not staying the same through innovation and technological advancement. They are not absolute and unchanging, not immutable, and thus not inhuman in that sense, but they are not human either. Human organisation might be seen to be a contradiction in terms as far as formal organisations go, but as Henri Bergson averred, organisation is a distinguishing sign that an organism is engaging with its environment – a sign of life (Linstead and Mullarkey, 2003). But it is equally true, as Gibson Burrell (1997) illustrates, that organisations themselves are bad for human beings in many ways – physically, psychologically, economically and politically. Is being human a flaw, or does it signal redemptive potential? Should we seek to protect ourselves from our humanity, or encourage it to flourish? Does being human allow us to claim rights over the planet or over other species, or does it disqualify us from such presumptions? Are there categories of the human that justify discrimination in the partitioning of these rights? Are some of us more human, and hence, in George Orwell's words, more equal than others?

Peter Norman is not a name that would enter human rights discourse as readily as the name of Martin Luther King would. Or even the names of Tommie Smith and John Carlos, the two American sprinters who won gold and bronze in the 200 metres at the 1968 Mexico Olympics, and stood on the podium in an iconic black gloved salute to raise global awareness of Black civil rights. This iconic pose was later concretised in a statue on the Stanford University campus, where the podium is reproduced, but with the second place step remaining empty. This was the step on which Norman, a White Australian, had stood. He had just set an Australian record that stands to this day almost 50 years later. And he wore a borrowed badge, that of the Olympic Project for Human Rights, as worn by Smith and Carlos. For this symbolic act he was never allowed to represent his country again, despite running qualifying times for the 200m 13 times and the 100m 5 times in 1972. Neither was he invited to be involved in the 2000 Sydney Olympic ceremonials, as he continued to refuse to condemn the actions of Smith and Carlos and retract his support for their cause – a strange insistence by the Australian Olympic Committee seemingly in spite of the fact that the sprinters had long since been reinstated by the USA. In 2012, the Australian Parliament formally apologised to Norman, but by this time he had been dead for six years. Smith and Carlos had carried his coffin.

Identifying as a human being against one's own sectional interests can thus be a high risk affair. Not only does one risk the ostracism of one's own group, but the group whose rights are being supported may ultimately also erase the outsider from their own memory, as with the Stanford statue. Being in sympathy with the persecuted or the suffering is not the same as being persecuted or suffering, even though personal persecution and suffering may well follow as a result of that alignment.

The lack of solidarity here may well have some justification. Responding as some have done to the Black Lives Matter movement in the USA has led to a reactionary counter-movement claiming that All Lives Matter because, essentially, we are all human. This misses the point – BLM are not claiming that no one else matters, but are using a slogan to draw attention to a particular sustained violation of the rights of their racial group that far exceeds anything being experienced, en masse, by other racial groups – because they are being treated by law enforcement agents across the country as inhuman, or sub-human. It is a matter of identity, as it was for Smith and Carlos, but not simply identity politics – and identity is an important prerequisite for claiming rights. According to Jacques Rancière (2010), under contemporary conditions of economic, cultural and political globalisation, specific resurgences of national and organisational 'identity' have displaced ethical considerations and occluded political processes that determine precisely who is allowed to have such things as human rights. Capitalist organisation is always human organisation, even where it seeks to reduce its dependence on what it defines as human 'frailty', or creates legalistic anthropomorphic fictions such as 'the corporation' to which it effectively accords human rights (Richardson and Cragg, 2010; Cragg, 2000, 2004). But it frequently also displays inhumanity towards those both outside and within it, which is not what we expect from supposedly ethical (and justifiable) systems. It measures and grades, qualifies and disqualifies, includes and excludes us. But even if we are unequal, don't we all still count as human? Who, or what kind of entities, have a say in defining the qualifying terms and delineating the boundaries? Who is marginalised or rendered invisible in these processes? Being fully and reflexively human, Rancière (2010) argues, requires an existential ambivalence to issues such as ethics, and a critical stance toward any moral authority that commoditises the 'good' in the interests of particular communities at the expense of others by abstracting and universalising it – using one community's specific interests to measure another. The pursuit of the absolute is by definition the pursuit of the inhuman. Being human necessitates being able to question what 'human' means.

Furthermore, defenders of the human rights of others may often in the process usurp or even exploit those rights in the process. For Rancière the wider voice of political critique has effectively been displaced by the appeal to an ethics in which ends entirely justify means that Jean Bricmont calls 'humanitarian imperialism'. As Rancière comments in relation to September 11th, 2001: 'The … manifesto issued by American intellectuals in support of George W. Bush's policies highlighted this point well: the United States are first and foremost a community united by common moral and religious values, an ethical community more than one of law and politics. The Good, by which the community is founded, is therefore the identity between law and fact. And the crime perpetrated against thousands of American lives can be immediately considered a crime perpetrated against the Empire of Good itself' (Rancière, 2002, p. 2–3; 2010, p. 75–76; Bricmont, 2008, 30–31).

Here the real 'people' who were the actual victims of a specific atrocity thus disappear in a process of becoming the 'absolute victim' – a non-specific victim that can encompass all races and peoples, a transcendental victim that is the victim of an infinite evil against whom the only conscionable response is infinite reparation. The apostrophised existence of infinite evil has thus become the justification for 'humane' war. Individuals, whose rights are supposed to be protected by an intervention under such auspices against this Evil, paradoxically lose their own human rights because, as a victim of an infinite evil, they are subsumed by an infinite fight greater than themselves – and consequently the party taking up that fight, ostensibly on their behalf, assumes their rights, absolutely, and so displaces them to a mere event in a historical chain of events. So 'the obligation of attending to the victims of absolute Evil has become identical to the fight without limits against this evil' (Rancière, 2002, p. 4; 2010, p. 77).

Infrahuman identities

Both victims and culprits can suffer under such a regime in which rights are customarily ceded to others, as attested to by the prisoners in Guantanamo Bay, where who was guilty and who was innocent remained undetermined indeterminately, as did the facts behind why they were brought and detained there. The relationship between identity and justice therefore becomes problematic. On the one hand identity is needed to claim certain human rights: rights that one has as a citizen of a particular country (the US, the UK) for example. But the counterpoint here is that an identity may be ascribed that renders one beyond rights (terrorist, Al Qaeda sympathiser, Taliban faithful, ISIS activist, fundamentalist, communist): neither human nor inhuman, but infrahuman, such that specific justice is impossible, and only infinite injustice can emerge, as permanent dispossession (Gilroy, 2004, p. 53).

An example not drawn from the era of the 'War on Terror' illustrates how pervasive this style of thinking is. On December 12, 1991, the following leaked internal memo was sent by Lawrence (Larry) Summers, at the time Chief Economist at the World Bank (and subsequently Secretary of State in the Clinton Administration 1999–2001, President of Harvard University 2001–2006, and Director of the National Economic Council under President Obama 2009–2010): 'I think the economic logic behind dumping a load of toxic waste in the lowest wage country is impeccable and we should face up to that. … I've always thought that under-populated countries in Africa are vastly UNDER-polluted; their air quality is probably vastly inefficiently low compared to Los Angeles or Mexico City. … The concern over an agent that causes a one in a million change in the odds of prostate cancer is obviously going to be much higher in a country where people survive to get prostate cancer than in a country where under-5 mortality is about 200 per thousand' (cited in Gilroy, 2004, p. 11).

The inhabitants of 'low-wage' countries are by this token attributed inefficient bodies of low worth, and as Gilroy (2004, p. 12) points out, there may be more than an echo of eugenics here that sees these worthless bodies as a form of 'planetary pollution'. They exist in a 'death zone' of high infant mortality and shorter lifespans, and they must bear some responsibility for their own situation because they are industrially inefficient. Low economic status is translated into low biological status and low biopolitical status. They have not earned and do not deserve the same human rights as those who have demonstrated superiority by colonising, ruling, enslaving, exploiting, indoctrinating, judging, imprisoning and when necessary executing them. Any behaviour that is different can be rendered abject; and anything abject is less than fully human (Banerjee, 2008).

The ascription of such infrahuman identities may also be popularly made by extension, on the basis of little or no evidence, to Blacks in general, or in the case of extremism and terrorism to Muslims in general, Afghans in general, Arabs in general, Jews in general, Romanies in general, or (pick one's favourite demonised group) in general. On the other hand, whilst the ascription of evil travels in one collective direction the ascription of virtue may travel in another: ethics may render the principles of law identical with the practices of a community (the US, the West, middle-class White males, Christians, the Tea Party), such that identifying with and being identified by that community allows it to write and prosecute its own 'bill of rights' as infinite justice. In the process such a normative community declares itself to be both good and human – with the self-defining capacity to determine the nature of either - to the extent that relational ontology and political critique are rendered irrelevant. Such practices cannot comprise a form of justice.

Of course, this denigration does not stop at evil. One can deny another rights in accord with any value that can be expressed absolutely, or inferred as absolutely non-negotiable. The ethical response to hurt, and even to atrocity, must therefore be an ambivalent one: not to deny the hurt but not to demand reparation, to remain open, not walled off – which would be to be inhuman. As Butler (2005, p. 103) puts it 'to be human seems to mean being in a predicament that one cannot solve ... if the human is anything it is a double movement, one in which we assert moral norms at the same time as we question the authority by which we make that assertion'. Because it lacks this ethical capaciousness, the absolute, and the idea of ethics as universal, cannot be human.

Humanity and identity

'We may not know what absolute good is or the absolute norm, we may not even know what man is or the human, or humanity – but what the inhuman is we know very well indeed' (Adorno, 2001, p. 175 cited in Butler 2005, p. 106).

'When one designates something as "human", one engages in a partitioning in which something else is immediately excluded from that categorisation and is immediately relegated to animality – the name, the category, the partition, the identity, even one that seems universal and open to every difference ... is always, above all else, a form of capture' (Adams, 2005).

When someone or some quality is designated as human, something other is simultaneously deemed to be outside that boundary: inhuman or animal, something less than or beneath the human: something infrahuman. The human stands beyond the nation, the group, the self; it is a quality that transcends the singularities that make us each inimitable, and the specific conditions of the co-constitution of each of our selves. The organisation and distribution of categories is also a distribution of inequality, the creation of moral maps if not moral hierarchies. For Foucault, the practices and institutions of categorisation are a form of subjectification, a means by which subjects, and from the point of view of the sovereign categorisers preferably docile subjects, are produced – creatively circumscribing the possibilities for their own creativity.

Rancière (1999, p. 35–42), however, argues that subjectification can have a more positive sense, in that in the assertion of a singularity or minoritarian classification as equal to identities already subjectified in the Foucauldian sense, an alternative subjectification can be achieved, as in the demonstration of equality one is able to become a subject. This becoming a subject is not so much becoming subject to (the police order) as becoming the subject of – making oneself appear (where categories had previously rendered one invisible), creating and impressing oneself on the scene that is, as Butler (2005, p. 9ff) argues, the scene of address that establishes the terms of the encounter with the Other (Adams, 2005). Indeed for Rancière the fact that the subject is a 'speaking' subject, even taking into account the critique of the idea of the phonocentric subject made by poststructuralism, is significant, as subjectification is: 'the production through a series of actions of a body and a capacity for enunciation not previously identifiable within a given field of experience, whose identification is thus part of the reconfiguration of the field of experience' (Rancière, 1999, p. 35).

Such a bearing witness depends on a prior capacity for negativity, a capacity for being impressed upon by the full range of experience, a quality that is important in poststructuralist thought (Linstead, 2000). The positive and creative subjectification so enabled however means dissociating one's identity from part of the classification of the 'police' order, reversing through action and discourse the inequality implied by that order and asserting equality. This dissensus is not simply a refusal though – it is a creative intervention which makes politics an aesthetic phenomenon, and Rancière re-emphasises this repeatedly (Rancière, 1999, 2002, 2004, 2009). It is a form of accounting for the self that changes the terms by which the self is accounted. This aesthetic approach to radical equality resonates with and extends the later Foucault (Rancière, 1999, p. 32), and Butler (2005, p. 133–134) captures the new light that this line of thought throws on the question of subjectivity, creativity and responsibility:

> [I]f ... new modes of subjectivity become possible, this does not follow from the fact that there are individuals with especially creative capacities. Such modes of subjectivity are produced when the limiting conditions by which we are made prove to be malleable and replicable, when a certain self is risked in its intelligibility in a bid to expose and account for the inhuman ways in which the 'human' continues to be done and undone ... the subject becomes a problem for moral philosophy precisely because it shows us how the human is constituted and deconstituted, the modes of its agentic self-making as well as its ways of living on. (Butler, 2005, p. 133–134)

The right to be human is reflexive, it would seem, as it crucially entails the right to develop and deconstruct the very constitution of that humanity. But for Rancière, historical and contemporary efforts to establish the 'Rights of Man' and 'Human Rights' have typically not encompassed this.

The human and the political

In Rancière, the connection between the human and the political is crucial. Politics begins with the sense of a wrong, just as ethics does for Butler and Adorno, but the ability to demand redress, even to voice one's sense of grievance, or simply to be able to speak and be recognised, is not granted to all. Rancière (1999) draws on Aristotle's distinction between the human and the animal, where humans are political precisely because they have the power of speech (which is, in effect, the claim to subjectivity). Speech enables them to render issues of justice and injustice into a common understanding, but animals can only voice feelings of pleasure or pain. Animals can indicate pleasure or pain with phône or noise; humans, commanding the logos through speech, express good and evil, usefulness or harmfulness, right and wrong, values and valuation.

Here Rancière distinguishes between mésentente, or disagreement, and Lyotard's (1988) concept of the différend, which he challenges. In the différend, two speakers may fail to achieve understanding because they use the same words, but each has a different referent that the words evoke. Because human experience is diverse and cannot be adequately contained in words, there will always be some inevitably impenetrable area where they cannot find agreement and understanding. Their genres of discourse and modes of phraseology will reflect this and embody this différend; to be entrapped in the wrong language is literally to be sentenced to misunderstanding. But a more radical misunderstanding is where one speaker cannot recognise the other as having intelligibility at all, and sees them only as voicing phône rather than logos. They are not taken seriously. They may be dismissed, and indeed suffer any kind of symbolic violence including demonisation, or they may be incorporated into society as useful tools but not legitimate members (as with the international case of migrant workers). They have no part in language, that quintessentially human product, and hence none in politics.

If some people cannot consider others as speakers, it is simply because they do not see them, because they don't have the same share within the political partitioning of the sensible (Deotte and Lapidus 2004, p. 78).

This position differs from that of Habermas, where human equality is a matter for discourse, achieved within communication by improving the emancipatory performativity of debate, rather than being a condition for access to the debate itself. Politics for Rancière (1999, p. 14, 30ff) begins when those regarded as having no voice, or no intelligence, or no part in this partitioning of the sensible (being 'the party of no part'), insist on being heard and introduce new phrases to designate themselves, to create a space for the recognition of their subjectivity and collectivity. They introduce the voice of feeling into the space of the logos and make it respond. They compel human reason to recognise the humanity of the other, and recognise their 'inhumanity' as human. As Rancière articulates:

> Politics is commonly viewed as the practice of power or the embodiment of collective wills and interests and the enactment of collective ideas. Now, such enactments or embodiments imply that you are taken into account as subjects sharing in a common world, making statements and not simply noise, discussing things located in a common world and not in your own fantasy. What really deserves the name of politics is the cluster of perceptions and practices that shape this common world. Politics is first of all a way of framing, among sensory data, a specific sphere of experience. It is a partition of the sensible, of the visible and the sayable, which allows (or does not allow) some specific data to appear; which allows or does not allow some specific subjects to designate them and speak about them. It is a specific intertwining of ways of being, ways of doing and ways of speaking. (Rancière, 2004, p. 10; 2010, p. 152)

Politics is therefore the space of the human, where humanity begins, as well as the space where bounded, arrogant, non-inclusive and oppressive versions of the human must founder. Rancière, in contrast to Lyotard (1991), is a communicative optimist, preferring an active hermeneutics of confidence to one of suspicion: he believes that we can knowingly recognise language's limitations whilst embracing its creative possibilities for action and change.

> [T]he specificity of politics springs from communicational stakes. For those who speak out 'politically' do not exist politically before this act of speaking out … that literally institutes a universe which, without it, would never have existed. A universe of the phrase comprises an audience, a destination, a meaning, a referent, all emerging from the fact of this phrase. … The political order, instituted by such phrases and sentences,

is a purely artificial device, and therefore contingent, a product made by the apparatus and the industry of the symbolic. (Deotte and Lapidus, 2004, p. 79)

This, as previously noted, makes politics an aesthetic activity, and initiates the question of the art of being human (Dobson, 2007; Foucault, 1973, p. 350). But a crucial consideration here, and central to the concerns of this book, is the construction of the not-human.

From inhumanity to evil … and back?

Rancière (1999) departs from Lyotard in his view of the impact of language and the nature of disagreement, but he is nevertheless influenced by Lyotard's idea of the inhuman as being split into two senses (Rancière, 2010, p. 73). The customary situations that we call 'inhuman' – cruelty, torture, deliberately occasioned distress, repression, slavery, machine-like bureaucracy – are not autonomous. Rather they are the consequences of our betrayal of another, alternate, 'good' Inhuman. This good Inhuman is (when capitalised) the principle of Otherness as such. It is that part in us that we do not control. It makes us who we are but it is not us. It may be the primary experiences of our birth and infancy which as Butler notes are 'unaccountable'. It may be whatever constitutes our Unconscious. It may be our individual reactions against, or suffered accommodation to, the Law. It may be our idea of a divinity, or spirit. Recalling Bataille, the 'inhuman' is excessive as it pushes us beyond what we comfortably embrace as our human limitations, and to engage with it requires excessive behaviour that always involves a degree of letting go and vulnerability even to the point of sacrifice – pursuing experience to and beyond its limits to the edge of a madness that could be ecstatic or horrific (Linstead, 2000). Intense spiritual or artistic insights into this state are often dearly bought through effort resulting in privation and exhaustion, and, insofar as they make it impossible to exist in the world as it is (the problem of dasein) result in depression even to the point of suicide. So we attempt to reduce them to a familiar and manageable level, in one of many possible aesthetic or conceptual forms of kitsch, to bring them under the auspices of specific rules of discourse (Linstead, 2002).

But as Otherness, the Inhuman is irreducible, Untamable, and it holds us hostage or slave. For Lyotard, to deny our situation as hostages, to fool ourselves that everything is at least potentially under our control and to dismiss our dependence on and the power of our Inhuman aspects, is to pursue the taming of the Untamable and to attempt to build a world that falls entirely under our mastery. This tendency can be seen in what Hardt and Negri (2000) also recognise as Empire, and it is for Lyotard the beginning of Absolute Evil, the appellation of which may be projected onto any forces that resist such moves to be controlled. The first step on the road to becoming absolutely evil is to not have, or to be denied, a voice: to be denied stories or have one's stories discounted, one's analogical identity dismissed or digitised. The road to incorporation, exemplified by the containment of the romanticised revolutionary potential of the Marxian proletariat within the domestications of the kitsch of Adorno's mass consumerism, is to have those stories displaced and remodelled into something less 'other', less alternative, to be granted only a humanity that is denied singularity.

Furthermore, as Corcoran (2010, p. 14) comments, the embodiment of absolute evil is a useful device for a warrior-state to generate a frightened collective of easily manipulated citizens, especially where the state is increasingly based on 'promoting the unbridled reign of the commodity'. But Rancière's argument is that the contemporary military export of 'liberal democracy' operates autonomously of the customary principles of economic or technological determinism by which commodity capitalism is legitimated, by resorting to an overriding principle of insecurity. As capitalism requires creative destruction, generating economic and personal insecurity, 'the most advanced form of the contemporary consensual state is that which requires the generation of new situations of insecurity to enforce its governance' because that insecurity is collective, and creates the collective as it redefines the human and inhuman (Corcoran, 2010, p. 14). To be neoliberally human then, means to be anxious. And anxiety drives out the impulse to care, to embrace, to be compassionate, to share vulnerabilities, and places limits on what we can learn.

Let's take an example. The contemporary phenomenon of 'philanthrocapitalism' (Bishop and Green, 2008) illustrates how this insecurity is operationalised in apparent opposition to the workings of the State, in an avowed distrust of what Rancière (1999) calls 'police apparatus' in relation to the efficient distribution of charitable donations, yet which polices a deeper consensus about markets, competition, global governance and the role of consumption in mediating the identity of the poor. Similarly, Bill Gates calls the work of the Bill and Melinda Gates Foundation 'creative capitalism'. The foundation is also heavily supported by Warren Buffett and has a capitalisation of around $60 billion USD, dwarfing the budget of even high-profile NGOs such as UNICEF, for example. Gates notes that 'There are markets all over the world that businesses have missed; the poorest two-thirds of the world's population have some $5 trillion in purchasing power', later adding that 'it would be a shame if we missed such opportunities' (Gates and Kiviat, 2008). Gates is heavily influenced by Prahalad (2004) and the debate is taken up, inter alia, by Edwards (2008, 2010).

Gates' argument is that the innovative qualities that made the rich corporations rich can be turned to providing inventive solutions to the world's human and social problems if the right incentives are there, and business operating principles can make the delivery of social welfare and third sector objectives more effective. Notwithstanding that evidence tends towards the contrary, and that business is often the source of the problems and the obstacle (e.g. via political lobbying) to public effectiveness in tackling them, the objectives are not new. Business continues to operate in the interests of shareholders and philanthropy is a form of long-term investment in the growth of new markets and new types of market, not a commitment to social and structural change, and certainly not change in the nature of capitalism (Richardson and Cragg, 2010). There is no public accountability, and no attempt to involve the recipients of 'aid' in any kind of process of self-determination. Living standards may be raised in specific respects, but at the cost of loss of autonomy and community development, and the image of companies doing virtuous work can lead to a relaxed approach to regulation, further weakening the sense of social responsibility and accountability for the public good. What happens is that capitalism demonstrates its plasticity and extends the scope of its policing of its core principles of competition, individual interest, profit, shareholder value, monetisation, short-term measurement of benefit and privatisation of resources into new areas, inscribing and incorporating new others into its political aesthetic, appropriating their rights and occluding their humanity whilst ostensibly acting in their unarticulated interest. Capitalism may assume a 'human' face, but it is an abstract face, the face of no particular human – a terrible face.

This book then collects a series of contributions to a philosophical anthropology of organisation. They locate that anthropology relative to key historical and contemporary thinkers. They take it down to the microlevel of everyday actions and affects. They remove its masks. They extend the question in the direction of technology. They wrestle with the politics of care. But most importantly, they see the vital importance of opening up the ambivalent space of being human, engaging in sharing their agreements and disagreements to keep the question of what it is to be human, open, alive and unsolved. For to fail to do this is to turn one's back on one's own humanity.

Note

1   Human (James Harris III [Jimmy Jam] and Terry Lewis) ©Flyte Time Tunes 1986

References

Adams, J. (2005) *Ma Luna A'eo Na Lahui a Pau Ke Ola o Ke Kanaka*, Online communication, 17th October.
Adorno, T. (2001) *Problems of moral philosophy*. Palo Alto, CA: Stanford University Press.
Banerjee, S. B. (2008) *Corporate social responsibility: the good, the bad and the ugly*. London: Edward Elgar.
Bishop, M. and Green, M. (2008) *Philanthrocapitalism: how the rich can save the world*. London: A.C. Black
Bricmont, J (2008) *Humanitarian imperialism: using human rights to sell war*. Trans. Diana Johnstone. New York, NY: Monthly Review Press.
Burrell, G. (1997) *Pandemonium: towards a retro-organization theory*. London: Sage.
Butler, J. (2005) *Giving an account of oneself*. New York, NY: Fordham University Press.
Corcoran, S. (2010) 'Introduction', in: Rancière, J. *Dissensus: on politics and aesthetics*. London: Continuum.
Cragg, W. (2000) 'Human rights and business ethics: fashioning a new social contract', *Journal of Business Ethics* 27(1–2), p. 205–14.
Cragg, W. (2004) 'Human rights, globalization and the modern shareholder owned corporation', in: T. Campbell (ed.) (2004), *Human rights and the moral responsibilities of corporate and public sector organisations*. Dordrecht: Kluwer, p. 105–28.
Deotte, J. -L. and Lapidus, R. (2004) 'The differences between Rancière's "Mésentente" (Political Disagreement) and Lyotard's "Différend"', *SubStance* 103, 33(1), p. 77–90.
Dobson, J. (2007) 'Aesthetics as a foundation for business', *Journal of Business Ethics* 72(1), p. 41–6.
Edwards, M. (2008) *Just another emperor? The myths and realities of philanthrocapitalism*. New York: Demos/Young Foundation.
Edwards, M. (2010) *Small change: why business won't save the world*. New York: Demos.
Foucault, M. (1973) *The birth of the clinic: an archaeology of medical perception*. Trans. A. M. Sheridan Smith. New York: Vintage Books.
Gates, B. and Kiviat, B. (2008) 'Making capitalism more creative'. *Time*, July 31.
Gilroy, P. (2004) *After empire: melancholia or convivial culture*. London: Routledge.
Habermas, J. (1984) *The theory of communicative action*. Boston: Beacon Press.
Hardt, M. and Negri, A. (2000) *Empire*. Cambridge, MA: Harvard University Press.
Linstead, S. A. (2000) 'Ashes and madness: the play of negativity and the poetics of organization', in: Linstead, S. A. and H. J. Höpfl (eds) (2000) *The aesthetics of organisation*. London: Sage, p. 61–93.
Linstead, S. A. (2002) 'Organizational kitsch', *Organization* 9(4), p. 657–84.
Linstead, S. and Mullarkey, J. (2003) 'Time, creativity and culture: introducing Bergson', *Culture and Organization* 9(1), p. 3–13.
Lyotard, J. -F. (1988) *The differend: phrases in dispute*. Minneapolis, MN: University of Minnesota Press.
Lyotard, J. -F. (1991) *The inhuman: reflections on time*. Cambridge: Polity.
Prahalad, C. K. (2004) *The fortune at the bottom of the pyramid: eradicating poverty through profits*. Englewood Cliffs, NJ: Prentice-Hall.
Rancière, J. (1999) *Disagreement*. London: University of Minnesota Press.
Rancière, J. (2002) 'Prisoners of the infinite', *CounterPunch*, April 30, www.counterpunch.org/2002/04/30/prisoners-of-the-infinite/ (accessed 4-4-2016).
Rancière, J. (2004) *The politics of aesthetics*. Trans. Gabriel Rockhill. London: Continuum.
Rancière, J. (2009) *Aesthetics and its discontents*. Cambridge, UK: Polity.
Rancière, J. (2010) *Dissensus : On politics and aesthetics*, (2010) (ed. and trans. Steve Corcoran). New York: Continuum.
Richardson, J. R. and Cragg, W. (2010) 'Being virtuous and prosperous: SRI's conflicting goals', *Journal of Business Ethics* 92, p. 21–39.

Preface

The term humanisation is often met with a lot of scepticism. Humanisation in its most basic sense means becoming more human or humane. First of all, this might seem a rather strong term to discuss processes of organisational improvement or development. Also, how can such a broad concept really be meaningful in everyday organisational practice? To some, the term seems more appropriate to humanitarian emergencies. Generally, it is easier to agree on what constitutes a loss of humanity (dehumanisation) than it is to state positively what humanity means. This anti-humanist reluctance to define the human has its roots in poststructuralist and postmodern philosophy and feminist and postcolonial studies that have criticised oppressing universalisms. From that perspective one might argue that the term assumes some image of the human as incomplete, lacking, failing. More specifically, that it assumes some people to be in need of civilisation. Taking Western colonial history and humanist Enlightenment philosophy into account, humanisation could betray the arrogance of a hegemonic, patriarchal belief that one is in the position to state what the human is, disqualifying and foreclosing the discussion about 'other' values. Why would one want to go back to such a problematic concept – humanisation?

In managing we are of course, besides many other things, driven by some objective standards that need to be met – some organisational goals for example. We want to get things done, whether it is raising profits, smoothing out communication processes, making people happier with their job, innovating, improving efficiency … In one way or another, most of our actions are driven by some intuition that something is worth doing or is supposed to be done. Whatever it is, we assess how to reach our goals. One look at the standard airport management book section and a dozen 'how-to' titles jump up with blueprints that promise help. In mapping out management strategies, assumptions are made about people and their potential. In other words, about what humans are. Assumptions are made for example about the balance between individuality and sociality, about how people make sense of their work, about how work within organisations is related to society at large, about the meaning of privacy, about creativity versus rules, responsibility, ethics … Management, and management literature, as Stephen Linstead also points out in the foreword to this book, assume some image of the human.

This is the area that philosophical anthropology is all about. What if underlying philosophical notions of humanity always drive us to manage organisations the way we do? And if they do, in what way should they be doing this? In this book we suggest that it is valuable and perhaps even necessary to discuss such assumptions about what it means to be human. Not doing so might actually make us vulnerable to exactly the kind of foreclosure of discussion just mentioned and leave no room for criticism. Speaking about humanisation invites one to take a step back from everyday immersion in management of everyday business and critically reflect on our basic values and views.

This is not a how-to book. Academics – most of them with ample management experience – were invited to explore what humanisation means to them and to their management practice. This explains the great diversity of the chapters. The authors give an account of what it means to be human in a philosophical anthropological way, and how organisational processes relate to this and do (or don't do) it justice. The first two chapters of this book are purely theoretical and they explore the two opposing positions on a continuum between two ways of seeing humanisation. Fernando Suárez-Müller gives a first sketch of what a systematic theory of humanisation would encompass. He contends that every living being has a (prototypical) dialogical capacity that constitutes its dignity. Humanisation would then mean organisational processes and changes that positively affect universal 'dialogical values' as tolerance, equality, willingness and an orientation on the common good. This perspective can provide explicit guidance to our ideals. Humanisation would mean such universal values are expressed and developed in local forms and context. Organisations themselves appear to be 'in dialogue' with stakeholders and these relationships could be assessed for expressing the dialogical values. As a theory of humanisation Suárez-Müller's work could be compared to internationally well-known humanist philosophers such as Nussbaum, who intends to define humanity with specific capabilities that can be expressed or inhibited. The opposite position of Ruud Kaulingfreks takes the uncertainty of being human as a starting point, suggesting the development of a careful sensibility to the implicit values that motivate us. According to Kaulingfreks a sensitive dialogue is needed for sense making to get a chance. He places his trust in the idea that people make sense of their life and work within specific and limited contexts, making it problematic to 'impose' more universal values because people need to develop meaning locally for their work to make sense. Both views are open to criticism as their strengths also constitute their vulnerabilities – explicitness could be experienced as too specifically filled in, the other could be too vague. But it seems clear that managers who strive for their and their employees' work to make sense use strategies that are built on (implicit) assumptions somewhere along this continuum.

There is a fundamental tension within the concept of humanisation, carefully negotiated by the variety of authors. They agree on the value of humanisation as a concept, and the need for discussing it and making humanisation a part of organisations. They also agree that to be human is to make sense of and give meaning to experiences and to develop potential. Humanisation and sense making (also in the way Weick uses it) are bound together. But sense making is always contextual, bound to specific circumstances and people. This means that even though – as Suárez-Müller does – a theory about the solid principles of humanisation can be given, no universal blueprints or models for organisational structures or work processes can be given. There is a fundamental restraint on imposing on others how to organise their organisation, but managers and employees need to make sense and experience the meaning of their activities. Although the theories in this book seem very different, at least in form, perhaps this difference is not fundamental. Whatever the case, as is clear above, the room for dialogue and sense making can be fought for with very different arguments.

The local origin of this book is the very small and very young officially humanist University for Humanistic Studies in Utrecht in The Netherlands. (Humanist counsellors, educators and organisational advisers are trained here, and the education is legally on the same footing as that of pastors and priests). To our knowledge Douwe van Houten

(1947–2010) was one of the first authors to introduce the idea of humanisation as 'the practical side of humanism' within an academic context, although it did not become one of the formal principles of education and research until 2001. Building on the work of Jaap van Praag, who was a founding father of contemporary Dutch organised humanism, van Houten looked for the possibilities of stimulating and developing a meaningful life in local practices for the great diversity of people within the context of Dutch society.

Humanisation as the practical side of humanism struggles with the same tensions traditionally negotiated by humanism. Humanism has been widely accused of repressive universality of its image of Man based on White, western, male characteristics. And yet humanism is also based on the Renaissance revival of interest for historicity and the embeddedness in traditions that opens the perspective of situatedness. The (hermeneutical) situatedness of human beings could also provide the ground for fighting harmful, repressive ideals of universality. Perhaps the current emphasis on some form of dialogue by many of the authors can be traced back to this sensitivity to context. Perhaps humanisation always assumes the need to work at understanding, at a convergence of horizons that is not self-evident. Many of the authors vehemently resist the dominant trend in organisations to let models and calculations dictate all processes and structures, filling all possible room for sense making that can only be contextual and impermanent.

In 1989 the University of Humanistic Studies was founded, with Douwe van Houten as its first vice chancellor. Its first orientation was practice based and focussed on empowerment studies and action research in the humanities and social sciences based on humanist inspiration. Humanisation within organisations was the special interest of a research group called Critical Organisation and Intervention Studies, which did research in sense making and humanisation in organisations. Topics like emergence and coherence, organisational development, authenticity, spirituality and personal narratives and the relationship between ethics and action were at the core of this program.

Humanisation has been heavily undertheorised as a concept. In all the publications by the research group, there has been a reluctance to pin down the meaning of humanisation in general terms. In books one can often only find the term a few times. Its implicit meaning can be abstracted from what is said about humanism – where notions such as dignity, freedom, dialogue and situatedness are foregrounded – and from how they deal with notions like sense making. Rather than functioning as a model or object of academic disputes the term has been used as a fertile ground, a motivating intuition, and applied in a specific circumstance like that of care, education, or the labour market. Every researcher applies the term differently and gives a renewed meaning to the term. The term indicates a kind of process of becoming more humane but it has never been worked out systematically. One of the aims of this book is to provide this systematisation together with reflections in which humanisation still remains implicit, as just described.

Coming from a background in critical organisation studies this book tries to show the reader what kind of positions regarding humanisation in organisations are possible. Before we finish this introduction by giving an overview of the book, a few remarks about methodology are in place. In many chapters reflections are combined with (auto) ethnography, which is trending within organisation studies because of its ability to show the specificity of a context, which suits this study as well. For example Anthonio in this book discusses how he used his personal experience as CEO to educate himself about what humanisation could mean in a forensic psychiatric institution, and de Lima constructed his idea of humanisation from his experience as manager during the HIV/AIDS crises in Brazil. Taking the embeddedness of the researcher into account could be seen as one way to make humanisation part of research, as a dialogue between one's personal involvement or values and the lived reality of the research area.

Overview of the book

The book begins with two philosophical reflections by Suárez-Müller and Kaulingfreks on what humanisation can mean for organisations in general. They will give a point of reference for the other chapters in order to understand why certain practices can be framed in these ways. In themselves these two chapters reflect on what is addressed within the philosophical debate on humanism. Both positions often resemble each other's interest in being able to set the ground for an open dialogue. While one is focussed on how to understand answers coming from a dialogue, the other focusses on the questions that might be addressed in the dialogue.

Suárez-Müller describes humanisation as the historical process of the increasing expression of humanity. He sketches an outline for a philosophical anthropology in which the capability of dialogue is essential and constitutive of dignity. Based on Habermas and Hegel, Suárez-Müller develops a transcendental structure of dialogue in which values such as freedom, non-violence, justification, responsibility and openness are central. A humanisation of society takes place when its organisations enlarge the possibility for individuals to develop these dimensions of dignity, which find an articulation in dialogical practices. A dialogical attitude also includes the behaviour of organisations as they interact with their stakeholders. The increasing expression of dialogical values in the structures of societies and in personal, professional and organisational relationships is the ongoing realisation of human dignity. Humanisation is thus both descriptive and normative. It is not only Suárez-Müller's description of what happens, but of what should happen. The idea of humanisation is thus fundamentally related to a broad concept of justice. Although the ideal of dialogue could seem too rational, the importance of lived experience is stressed. Humanisation in this sense connects Romanticism with Enlightenment.

In the last chapter of this book, Suárez-Müller and Felber will combine the theory outlined in Suárez-Müller's chapter to write their story about what humanisation would mean for the economy. In the chapters by de Lima and Anthonio these ideas are put into practice.

Kaulingfreks philosophical approach is very different. He questions the question, put forward by this book, about what humanisation is. Coming from a perspective imbued with aesthetics he looks for what people find meaningful in their lives. He finds intuition to be a crucial notion, one that is also important for the chapters by Simons and Schreurs. According to Kaulingfreks, intuition deals with meaning while the intellect deals with the world at large and is therefore very handy to organise stuff. With Bergson he claims that we need intellect in order to act but we need intuition in order to have meaning. Intuition has no words but leads and pushes intellectual knowledge in a certain way that tells us if something 'is right' or not in an implicit way. The same applies to his notion of humanisation. Trying to deal with this notion intellectually brings him to a loss. He argues that there is a value in the unclearness of the concept. Not everything can be well defined and when we make things distinct we tend to forget about them. We only think according to Kaulingfreks when things are unclear, when there is doubt, when we are not sure what something is. Usually established definitions tend to become rules and regulations, which are very handy for administrators but end all discussion on what people find worth doing. The intuitions are not given, they develop and change because we keep thinking and discussing. To Kaulingfreks there is a kind of *paideia* or education going on. In a conversation meaning appears and a certain understanding becomes manifest. So although talking is as important to Kaulingfreks as it is to Suárez-Müller, it takes on a completely different status – it is all about implicitness, about intuitions that make sense as long as they are *not* expressed into essential structures. When we talk about humanising organisations it is about creating a sensibility for the value and meaning of humanising, not about knowing what humanising is. It is about the creation of a human value within the organisation in whatever shape or content it can take, before intuitions become incorporated into the goals of the organisation and closed for discussion. It is from this sensibility that we can act and discuss and by doing so we can search for humanisation.

The other chapters in this book all focus on a specific case representing a certain industry. There are two on education, one on health care, one on public service, one on consultancy, one on economics and one on the advertising industry. The order of the chapters was chosen to go from uncertainty to clarity, from perspectives that are closest to Kaulingfreks work to Suárez-Müller. We would not be surprised however, should clarity not be attained, because the more one reads, the more one might see how perspectives actually overlap.

Simons' story brings us into the realm of the consultants. What he claims is that consultants should not give answers to questions in an organisation but raise more questions. Consultancy should still be about *consultare*, discussing. Consultancy has the potential to contribute to humanisation if it digs deeper into what concerns people in specific circumstances. This is not common practice. When problems are detected, they are swiped off the workplace as soon as possible. In organisations and in mainstream organisation literature problems are not worth existing and are solved (stashed) as soon as possible, leading to new, 'wicked' problems. Consultants ignore problems that are complex, social and personal and 'solve' them by applying models and schemes based on existing, technical, impersonal knowledge, copying results of best practices elsewhere. To Simons this ignores and reduces problems, as much in quantity as in quality. There is no attention to the problems that are worth problematising. Counterintuitive as it may sound, knowledge creation in organisations to him is more about *living the problem* than finding solutions. In knowledge creation, *problematisation* is the most important event. He illustrates this by showing how *inexperienced* consultants start discussions, ask questions, and in this way problematise problems, questioning taken for granted beliefs and thus creating room for *new* insights to appear. Real knowledge creation in organisations appears when problems are taken seriously. In knowledge creating – or learning – the professional dilemmas, problems and tensions of communities are critically discussed. Problematisation to him is a humanising process that hears and gives voice to different professional experiences.

In the next chapter, by the editors van de Klundert and van Boeschoten, education is used as an example to illustrate a theory of humanisation in which technology has a central role to play based on Stiegler's philosophical anthropology. Human beings have always depended on socially developed and cultivated technics to live. There is no essence, human nature or activity, no transcendental subject. There is a fundamental uncertainty about what it is to be human, because it can always develop into new life forms, cultures and ways of living when imagination is used to learn new skills. Technics is our medicine, making autonomy possible, when there is a balance between the individual, the social and the technological (humanisation). However this cure can become a poison when it turns into addiction or when we are subjected to ever new technologies without having the time to become skilled, imaginative and thus autonomous in using them (dehumanisation). Clearly, different disciplines – such as managing and educating – entail differences in skills and in imagination of ideals. In other words, the differences between management and educators – and the tensions these cause – could be explained by looking at the technologies/skills used. We contend that in contemporary education, imagination based in information and communication technology (ICT) has become too dominant. (This is similar to what Schreurs identifies as the impact of new public management). The specific characteristics of ICT speak to managers about transparency and efficiency, translated into systems of control. Improved ICT promises more and more efficiency, but educators do not get the time to adopt such technologies to become skilled in their use. The skills, techniques and imagination needed to educate are different from those needed by management, which are mainly meant to administrate. Chances for humanisation in education should be looked for in starting the dialogue about such differences, recognising them and carving out the time and opportunities for making them contribute to one another. This chapter does not offers practical how-to tips but is meant to invite one to a new perspective on the basis of many tensions within organisations. It could be related to the chapter by Simons, in as far as we also suggest that a central problem in organisation is that the time needed for understanding and learning is not given.

Schreurs' interest is focussed on the dehumanising aspects in contemporary education. Everything in education seems to have become organised according to preset targets that are formulated as Specific, Measurable, Acceptable, Realistic and Time specific (a notion Kaulingfreks discusses as well). Schreurs states that in our meritocratic society targets seem essential for recognition. Since the formulated targets are not related to any kind of content, most of these targets are purely formal, procedural. This to him can be seen as a consequence of new public management. Students are seen as clients and become objective targets for the organisation. This is a problem in education since learning is based on interpersonal trustworthy relationships between students and teachers. Relationships and processes of learning and growth have an inherent element of uncertainty. The current trend is focussed on excluding this while to Schreurs it is one of the fundamental principles of humanity and human freedom – and should thus have its space in education. Uncertainty is part of the relation between teachers and students but also part of the way management in education should operate. Here the notion of paideia comes to mind as an open way of learning, which later in the German Romantic tradition led to the term Bildung. In order to humanise education Schreurs indicates that it is essential to reflect on the goals and values imbedded in education. Question that are central to him are: How can teachers instruct their students to deal with change and uncertainty and how can managers in education create enough room for these teachers to organise this? What is needed in contemporary education to break the chains of control and risk avoidance and make room for the wisdom of uncertainty?

The chapter by Anthonio and van de Klundert is based on Anthonio's experience as executive manager of a forensic psychiatric clinic. All public institutions deal with varying degrees of asymmetry in the relation between the person (client or patient) and the structure of the organisation. Government regulations limit the individual's ability to have control over one's own life, even though such institutions often intend to support and develop such an ability. The asymmetrical exercise of power, as Anthonio found out, is often experienced by both clients or patients and by staff to be humiliating and alienating. The authors contend that humanisation in organisations offers an alternative to over-regulation and unnecessary restriction of human dignity. These types of public or (semi-)

public organisations should stand at the service of the public and human values should be the guiding and regulating thought of the policy of the organisation and its implementation. No preset balance between horizontality and verticality can be given. Humanisation is an ideal that cannot be mapped out in advance and yet it can be a guiding principle for management. They show how management used a horizontal way of communication (Habermas) that gave clients and staff the opportunity to express their concerns, leading to an ideal that was shared by all and giving a clear direction for development towards an organisation that was experienced as more humane. They also show how theoretical sources can be used to guide such a process. Such sources helped management to question themselves during the changes. By using authors such as Goffmann, Margalit and especially Foucault they warn us that an ideal of humanisation can turn back on itself. Opposite to intentions, it is always possible that a repressive discourse about 'humane' values comes to completely cover and terrorise the organisation. As a manager Anthonio questioned himself, wondering whose humanisation is central to these institutions.

Millan Caceres looks at humanisation from within the advertising industry, which has been her main line of work over the last ten years. Humanity and human concerns to her are very much daily practice within this market. The belief system in most advertising agencies is that they need to relate to society, to people, to be inspired and to keep their creativity. That is why they call themselves agencies and not corporations. To Millan Caceres 'being in touch' with what goes on in society is adamant for creating good services. This is even more so since the use of social media has become obligatory. These technologies have reversed the *panopticon* of older power structures into a *synopticon*, where good advertising is actually dependant on really listening and engaging with different audiences. This also results in the blurring of personal and professional life, which under conditions of *liquid modernity* (as described by Bauman) again becomes an opportunity to engage with others and yourself in a more profound way. She will show this based on her own experiences. The conditions of *liquid modernity* fit well with this industry, which has always known great flexibility. With liquid modernity and new media people need to adapt all the time and have to challenge their way of looking at their social network. To Millan Caceres the advertising industry succeeded in taking up this challenge and using its humanising potential by managing the new kinds of relationship between clients, consumers and the corporations in a manner that could be an example to other industries. In the ad industry, instead of bureaucratisation, employees and management manage the *liquid environment* by creating flexible, human-based policies and human-based work environments. Millan Caceres contends that as liquidity takes over, it will be human relationship development that helps companies to survive.

De Lima discusses his experience as a health care administrator in Brazil during the HIV/AIDS outbreak crises. What he exemplifies is the need for all concerned to be in a dialogue so that it becomes clear how power relations frame possibilities for solutions in such a crisis. Humanisation to him is this organisation of the dialogue. HIV/AIDS is a complex issue where medical problems are entwined with social, political, economical and other issues. They all have their own form of understanding, their own voice by means of patients, doctors, institutions, family and others. De Lima uses Foucault to show that knowledge is power, especially in the medical world. Health care organisations reduced the problems to how they could organise 'medical' care as they saw fit. In health care organisations – as in society at large – the first to be excluded from the discussion and silenced were the ones about whom the discussion was centred: the patients. This is a form of dehumanisation to de Lima that needs to be counteracted. He states, based on Luhmann, that a reduction of complexity is the first response for organisations faced with new problems. Information is collected and structured to organise manageable flows. A resolution can be found by rationally reconstructing the complexity in such a way that all different interest groups are again involved in dialogue. So, by using Habermas similar to the way that Suárez-Müller does, de Lima finds the humanising solution in working environments in the way we use language and open up for debate with others. Communicative action based on equality grounds the humanistic approach according to de Lima and Suárez-Müller. Humanisation to both is about the creation of space where different voices can meet and participate.

In the last chapter of this book we round the circle with Felber and Suárez-Müller's discussion of a humanisation of the current economic system, based on Suárez-Müller's theory of humanisation and Felber's work on ethics for a new economy. One of the dialogical values with regard to the humanisation of economics is 'cooperating for the benefit of the common good'. They state that contemporary strong competitive markets have no room for a common good. Although our modern economic system of free competition (capitalism) is not formally built on violence and fear, as was once slavery and serfdom, competition nonetheless constitutes an organisational model in which these unethical values are very much alive for them. Felber and Suárez-Müller make it clear that it is possible to humanise the economy if we take cooperation instead of competition as its central organising principle. The ethical values of dialogue need to be integrated in all possible layers of the economic system. In an economy that deserves to be called *humane* these ethical values determine the rules of the game. The Greeks called the science of the household 'oikonomía', and its specific values were sharing and responsibility. Felber and Suárez-Müller relate these values to what has been the ground for our modern Western society since the French revolution: liberty, equality and fraternity. These should again be the leading point of reference for economies. Felber and Suárez-Müller exemplify that all kinds of measures can really be taken by discussing an organisation called *Economy of the Common Good*.

Acknowledgements

We would like to thank the University for Humanistic Studies for giving us the opportunity to work on this book. It has been a pleasure to work with Gower Publishers, especially our editors Kristina Abbotts and Sara Hutton, who are very precise and always very quick in their responses to our concerns. We would also like to thank everyone who has participated in the project that led to this book, of whom we would like to name specifically Isolde de Groot, Bram van de Klundert, Hugo Letiche, Ruud Meij and Radha Nandoe; and also Hans Alma, Daniel Blondelle, Sylwin Cornielje, Joep Delsasso, Arwen van de Gugten, Jean-Luc Moriceau, F.A. Muller and Evelien Tonkens. Thanks for your enthusiasm and intelligent contributions and comments. We would like to thank all contributors to this book for their positive and open support in making this project successful. We are thankful to Kees van de Velde, to whom we owe the beautiful cover he made using his own artistic work.

A special word of thanks to Bram and Yvonne van de Klundert, on whose critically constructive and patient support Myrte gratefully relied to be able to produce this book during her masters education. We dedicate this book them and to Robert's children, Tiber and Vianne.

Diemen/Rotterdam, January 2016

1 The process of humanisation[1]

Fernando Suárez-Müller

Introductory remarks

This paper develops a first sketch of what could be called a general theory of humanisation. (1) I will start by making a distinction between 'humanisation' understood as a mere activity of individuals or groups (it is in this sense that Douwe van Houten, one of the initiators of a general theory of humanisation, uses the concept) and 'humanisation' understood as a historical process taking place at different levels of society. (2) I will then consider the philosophical presuppositions and foundations of such a theory in order to show that humanisation presupposes the possibility of a *universal* ethics that is already a subject of philosophical research. (3) This will enable us to understand that humanisation is about both open and closed societies, and (4) that the specific case of a humanisation of organisations must be understood in the light of a historical dynamics that involves profound institutional changes.

Humanisation as an activity and as a process

The concept of 'humanisation' is often used in the sense of an activity.[2] It refers to the activity of actors contributing to the creation of a more humane world. 'World' has a wider sense than 'society' and in this wide sense it means that humanity cannot be the only object, the only *terminus ad quem* of humanisation, because other living beings and, in a derived way, natural organisations (ecosystems, the biosphere, the earth itself) can also occupy the place of the object. In our era it is not too hard to imagine that a more humane world would also include an ecological dimension.[3] When it comes to the ultimate *termini ad quem* of humanisation we should not only speak about humans but rather about rightholders in general.

It is possible to make a distinction between activities taking place on the micro-, meso- or macro-level of society. The micro-level of humanisation constitutes activities concerning individuals either as subjects or objects (recipients, rightholders) of humanisation. Individuals are the ultimate rightholders and therefore objects of humanisation at all levels of society (organisations and institutions on higher levels only have derived rights), but they are not, as I will argue, the only rightholders. At the micro-level, the actor is always an individual person. Humanisation here is concerned with the reflective control that actors have over their own actions. It is at this level that individuals give direction to their own reflective processes and actions. In the philosophy of the last decades of the 20th century this dimension was given a strong impetus by the works of Michel Foucault (1984a, 1984b) and Charles Taylor (1989). These authors however do not use the concept of humanisation because for them the general commitment to a more humane world presupposes a positive interpretation of a determinate sphere of values which should be filled in by the individual subjects themselves without there being any need for a general theory of humanisation. These authors prefer to speak of an 'ethics of the self', but they address this 'ethics' within large cultural and historical considerations that in fact belong to the macro-level of humanisation (Foucault, 1984b, p. 51–86; Taylor, 1989, p. 25–52). The structure of the hermeneutic circle, which was clarified by Hans-Georg Gadamer, characterizes the way in which Foucault and Taylor conceive their 'ethics of self' (Gadamer, 1990, p. 270–80). This concept takes the self to be both the actor and the *terminus ad quem* of humanisation.

At the meso-level the actor is a human organisation which, in the sense I am using the term here, has a very wide range from two-person associations to very large institutions. A human organisation is an acting body primarily constituted by the people working in it. The *terminus ad quem* of humanisation is always formed by the specific rightholders or stakeholders involved with the activities of the organisation (a customer, an employee, a citizen, a stock- or shareholder, an eco-system, etc.). Strengthening the normative basis of people working inside organisations, which has been called 'normative professionalization' (Jacobs, 2008), could be one specific strategy of humanising organisations. Another strategy of humanisation could be to restructure the organisation itself with the purpose of creating a more humane working environment and a more respectful use of nature (since not all rightholders are humans). This of course applies to all human organisations, including institutions that are social organisations embodying core values of society and having a relatively stable existence. Institutions are the pillars of society, while other organisations (associations, clubs, companies, research institutes, etc.) have a shorter lifetime. In general, organisations are more dynamic: they can also easily adopt an international extension. Institutions however provide a powerful means of restructuring other organisations. The state as an overall institution is a recursive (self-centred) body that, by means of government, is constantly changing society's own constitution thereby largely determining the dynamics of society. Again, individual rightholders are the ultimate object of all humanising activities.

The macro-level, as I am using the term here, concerns the historical dynamics of culture. Culture is the whole set of ideas that transform our mentality and these are mainly based on reflective processes carried out by art, religion and philosophy (including science). These reflective processes progressively transform society, the changes being both bottom-up and top-down. The macro-level conveys the idea of what I call the 'process character of humanisation' (and of course affects the other levels of society). Actions on the macro-level concern humanity and are of historical importance, but this does not mean that all people are actually involved in these actions. It means that such an action or process contributes to social changes, giving a deeper understanding of what we call 'human dignity'. The actions and processes taking place within a general cultural and historical process are steps towards a society in which on the one hand, people get all the opportunities required to develop independently their ideal (potential, true and legitimate) self, and in which on the other hand, people do justice to all entities considered to have fundamental rights. It is clear that the macro-level of humanisation cannot be separated from the image of an ideal society (a so-called 'utopia'), even though this image may be very basic, vague or general. Those who want to describe humanisation (or dehumanisation) as a cultural and historical process must methodologically presuppose such an ideal imagery. The idea of humanisation must therefore be complemented by a philosophical grounding of social and normative ideals of what humanity is.

Summarising, we may say that the micro-level of humanisation is based on humanising activities made possible by individuals, the meso-level concerns activities made possible by organisations in a broad sense (including institutions) and the macro-level concerns humanising activities affecting historical and cultural processes of socialisation.

Philosophical foundation of the process of humanisation

In the sense stated above, humanisation means that we have a more or less elaborated idea of what progress in cultural history could be, of those elements strengthening the essential characteristics of humanity. The idea of a desirable society depends on our perception of humanity. A theory of humanisation needs to be complemented by a philosophical anthropology. Although complementary, such a philosophical anthropology must be distinguished from biological and cultural anthropologies, which are only descriptive, because it focuses on human characteristics that are both *essential* and *normative* when it comes to formulating the idea of a desirable society. Neither biological nor cultural anthropology transcends the empirical domain unless they add a philosophical step. A philosophical anthropology on the contrary focuses on normative aspects related to humanity's essence. Those characteristics are essential which, once developed, give people their full humanity. To renounce the development of these abilities would cause an *alienation* from the human ideal, from an existence that is worth pursuing. A certain cultural development is necessary in order to allow human potential to prosper. So, we need to presuppose a more or less articulate conception of a desirable society or world.

Anthropologically, what differentiates humans is based on the idea that people are capable of moral insight, capable of thinking and acting in terms of rights and dignity. These fundamental characteristics are linked to our capacity for abstract thought. The most important *differentia specifica* of humans is not so much the ability to act morally, as it is the capability of articulating moral insights. *Homo sapiens* is a product of biological evolution but there is also a cultural evolution started by earlier hominids. *Homo erectus* knew how to use relatively sophisticated tools and mastered fire. These first human beings must also have possessed a relatively well-developed capability of abstract thought and a primitive form of speech. These cultural developments contributed to the success of the human species. Cultural processes not only influenced, but in fact determined by natural selection. Humankind is not only a product of natural evolution, it is also a product of a self-initiated cultural process. Hominisation was at some point in history part of the humanisation process. We know that *homo sapiens* buried their dead ritually, that they possessed such a level of abstract thought that they could deploy the imagery of the 'double world', adding transcendent beings to their view of reality (Leroi-Gourhan, 2006, p. 145–56). *Homo sapiens* is a being that lives in a deep (vertical), and not in a flat (horizontal) world.

This highly developed capacity of abstract thought determines other essential properties, which are typically human (Leroi-Gourhan, 1964). The influence of abstract thought on feelings, on the emotional or affective dimension, is crucial. And this can be characterised as a deepening of the world. Although rationality and feelings are often considered to be opposites, the deepening of the internal experience, of feelings and emotions, is, as Antonio Damasio has argued, reinforced by abstract thought and reason (2006, p. 127–64). The development of abstract thought, verbal language and deep emotionality could not but affect the social manifestations and constructions of humans. Abstract thinking and verbal interactions make a concomitant development of specialised powers possible (Dewey, 2000, p. 166–207; Jonas, 1997, p. 162–94). Abstract thinking and language seem to be based on an inner 'communicative and dialogical capacity' that has its deep origin in life, making cooperation and sociality possible.

This anthropology brings us to consider the ontological foundation of our abilities to think in an abstract way. What do we need, philosophically, to presuppose and enable these abilities? Several philosophers and biologists indicate that there is in life a proto-dialogical power at work. Jonas suggests that it is possible to define life as the proto-dialogical ability of a 'Self' deploying a hermeneutical relationship with its environment (Jonas, 1992, p.11–34; Bauer, 2008; Morin, 2008, p. 703–04). This 'Self' would be a bundle of cognitions, skills and desires which are all used in an interpretative and 'inner dialogical' relationship with the world. As has already been made clear by Maurice Merleau-Ponty, the process of perception presupposes the existence of a communicative relationship with an environment, setting aside the level of consciousness of the self (Merleau-Ponty, 1945, p. 228–32). It is clear that this demarcates a very speculative domain of philosophical biology. But there is nothing that precludes a further deepening of philosophical speculation recognising dialogical structures even in the centre of being itself, in which these structures become more and more explicit from the moment that life – and eventually the human mind – appears.[4] In this sense dialogue would be a very profound metaphysical principle constituting the ultimate grounding of the idea of humanisation.

Basically, the concept of humanisation combines a descriptive with a normative perspective and this is only possible as long as we are prepared to legitimate and ground our normative assumptions. A philosophical anthropology reconstructs essential human features as a compound of descriptive and normative elements. Abstract thinking, language, dialogue, reflection, rationalised feelings and self-consciousness are properties that define important aspects of our essence, and they are in themselves intrinsically dynamic. These properties have in fact an intrinsic desire of development. Their interrelatedness constitutes a dialogical power characterised by a will to understand and to unfold understanding. But this being said, we have still not grasped where this unfolding dynamic is heading. There exists an intrinsic connection between this dialogical power on the one hand and the determination of justice on the other. The dialogical faculty leads to the discovery of the domain of rightholding entities. This is an important insight made possible by the theory of communication of German philosophers like Karl-Otto Apel (1973) and Jürgen Habermas (1981), and their successors Dietrich Böhler (1992) and Rainer Forst (2007). Dialogue activates a set of normative principles that are essential to ground human rights. These principles are, as Apel explains, 'transcendental structures of dialogue', in fact normative ideals, constituting a necessary *a priori* condition for real dialogue. They are enacted from the moment that we are involved in communicative action. Important normative ideals implicit in this transcendental domain are: symmetry, equality, liberty, openness, peace (renouncement of violence), tolerance, respect, solidarity, cooperation, helpfulness, responsibility, recognition and reciprocity. This is not to be taken as an exhaustive list, since there could be more, and surely many others can be derived from them. These moral values are transcendental ideals and are automatically activated once an imagined or real dialogue starts (although the actors need not be conscious about their existence). Humankind derives its characteristic dignity from its strongly developed dialogical nature.

If a society does not do justice to this *idealism of dialogue* we may suspect that human dignity is endangered. The mass of entangled social and cultural processes that lead to the recognition of the existence of human dignity is one of the main development lines of humanisation. Dialogical idealism not only constitutes the philosophical basis of human dignity, it also constitutes the basis of the idea of human rights. Where human rights are at stake, we invoke human dignity as an expression designating a constellation of transcendental ideas guiding the dialogical mind. Because our dialogical power is innate, these ideas are also innate. They are both regulative and constitutive, and in fact *directive* (in a very specific teleological sense). The social and cultural circumstances in which communication takes place can preclude an effective realisation of these ideas. As long as they are not yet realised they remain ideals shaping the mind of visionary people. It should be possible to trace back all rights expressed in the *Universal Declaration of Human Rights* to one basic right to participate in free dialogue. Even such a fundamental right as the right to live gets its validity from a possible participation in the dialogical processes of society. This right to participate in dialogue also has an individual moral sense since dialogue is a means to develop one's own *moral essence* (one's own ideal *alter ego*). But it has a larger moral meaning since it is also a means to develop a *universal moral community*. The right to free dialogue is intrinsically connected to the fundamental right to be part of this *becoming community* that in the scope of our earthly limitations remains, as Maurice Blanchot would say, unavowable (1983). In terms borrowed from Robert Brandom (1994, p. 643), humanisation could be expressed as being a process of *making it explicit*, of *transposing* the implicit normative contents of discourse into a real moral community. Human dignity is then conceived to be an *intrinsic* value.

According to this picture, human rights are implicitly contained in humankind's essence, in its being and nature. But an extended version of the concept of dialogue (as the inner structure of mind and consciousness) can also explain, I think, the controversial idea of an *intrinsic* dignity of animals. The concept of dignity is polyvalent because nature shows different levels of consciousness and thus different levels of communicative and expressive faculties. This can give us an indication of what the 'intrinsic value of life' could mean, making a *jus animalium* possible. Such a picture, of course, presupposes a *scala justitiae*, a gradual repartition of rights. The idea of a *scala justitiae* fundamentally challenges the modern image of nature, since nature here is identified with a normative dimension showing a cosmic unfolding of rights.

Opening and closing society

Socio-cultural processes that have helped humanity to develop societies respecting human rights constitute important steps of humanisation. Democratisation is just one line of humanisation. The goal of an open society, as conceived by Karl Popper (1971), is a society that encourages free and open communication. On the political level this involves the realisation of a system of general participation in power. But it also involves the development of other domains. An open society can be perceived as having three strands: the social dimension of power, the objective dimension of meaning (knowledge), and the subjective dimension of happiness. An open society however can also be considered to be closed when it comes to protecting the rights of individuals and larger organisations (states, communities, but also eco-systems, seas, landscapes, etc.). Being closed here implies a clear demarcation of the boundaries for rightful action.

The concept of humanisation, as considered above, includes the idea of a civilisation process of humanity. There is a strong future-oriented connotation thanks to the concept's implicit idealistic content that cannot be separated from a certain (more or less articulated) utopianism. After finishing the process of decolonisation, the concept of civilisation got a bitter aftertaste. However, in *Civilización y barbarie* the postcolonial Argentinian thinker Domingo Sarmiento (2003) still uses the concept in a positive sense denoting enlightenment, democratisation and modernisation. Unlike the flat notion of culture the more vertical concept of civilisation expresses the idea of a civilised understanding of articulate citisens who in a versatile way work on both their personal formation (Bildung) and social justice. As a concept humanisation opens the possibility of accommodating this positive meaning of civilisation, without incorporating any sentiment of superiority or fear of uniformity, because the concept is connected with a dialogical space that can only be thought of as being pluralistic. In this sense the German sociologist Norbert Elias gives us an idea of what civilisation as humanisation can mean, connecting institutions, people's attitudes and the development of individual personalities with large cultural changes. He emphasises the process character of civilisation by using the word 'Zivilisierung'. In this process manners become more refined, and personal behaviour becomes rationalised and psychologised, thereby creating a growing aptitude to empathise with others (Elias, 1976, p.74). It is clear that rationalisation does not mean instrumental rationalisation. It refers to a growing ability to develop a pronounced sense of responsibility for humanity and all rightholding entities as was described later by Hans Jonas (1992).

The term 'enlightenment' needs some clarification. Enlightenment is a learning process that allows humankind to improve its reflective and communicative capacities. As is already the case in the definition given by Immanuel Kant (1964), this task of empowerment of humans must be connected with the idea of liberation from alienation. As Max Horkheimer and Theodor Adorno (1981) have shown, the process of enlightenment itself involves a strong element of alienation. This line of critique goes back to Jean-Jacques Rousseau and especially to the Hegelian idea of alienation. These ideas do not really affect the definition given by Kant, to whom enlightenment is all about liberation from the alienation that follows from humanity's self-incurred immaturity ('selbstverschuldete Unmündigkeit'). In this light, the development of humankind's reflective and dialogical capacities seems to be the only real antidote to alienation. The process of enlightenment can therefore be redefined as the realisation of a society that does justice to human essence, to our dialogical nature. Kant presupposes that humanity is able to overcome its immaturity by breaking down those structures hindering free dialogue. If liberty means that we need to create enough space for dialogical processes, responsibility means that we are the only living beings capable of carrying out this process of liberation. Humankind must actively gain mastery of its own destiny. Responsibility, therefore, means to be open to the imperatives of individual formation (Bildung) and collective moral development. A theory of humanisation however must be larger than this Kantian picture of enlightenment because it also has to take into account the shadow-sides of modernisation. If we interpret this process of enlightenment as liberation of the space of communication, as progressive realisation of the 'idealism of dialogue', the strong opposition between rationality and affectivity, of enlightenment and romanticism disappears. Humanisation therefore also includes a process of *romantisation*. The emotional and affective side of the human mind is not opposed to rationality but is in fact part of it, as has been shown by Habermas, who includes emotional truthfulness and authenticity (*Wahrhaftigkeit*) in the realm of communicative rationality (1981, p. 324). Humanisation does not only stand for 'potentiating dialogical structures in human society', it also involves a growing sensibility towards the expressiveness of the natural world. The new humanism involved here is capable of saying: 'Nihil animalium mihi alienum puto!'[5]

The process of humanisation

Humanisation presupposes the idea of progress. This progress can be measured along several lines. In the political domain it accomplishes a transition from an authoritarian system of command in ancient closed societies to a form of government that allows participation in modern open societies – thus dialogical principles increasingly become the organisational principle of society. Historically speaking, this progress need not be a linear and necessary process. There is not just one clear-cut series of events making such an open society possible. But there is a certain 'logical necessity' behind the events because certain steps, like the creation of a state of law, a representative democracy, a welfare state, etc., are necessary points of orientation in order to be able to speak of progress. Transitions towards a higher level of humanisation can appear to be temporarily or permanently blocked. From a theory of humanisation these kinds of situations can be explained as processes of alienation. The democratisation process that started in the nineteenth century could well have been annihilated by the rise of authoritarian systems, and the ecological transformation of our modern democracies may end up in stagnation. But this does not alter the *logics* of progress.

As I mentioned before, humanisation can be measured along three basic lines. An open society should (a) promote a maximum of participation in power. This power must ultimately be thought of in terms of a global democracy involving all existing humanity and representing all rightholders (human or not). Real democracy is not just a matter of giving people a vote. There definitively is a 'will to act' or a 'will to power', but power can never be an end in itself; it should be accompanied by the development of a moral community.

Humanisation also means (b) maximising participation in knowledge (depending on talents and interests) in order to enable each individual to explore the meaning of life. Social and political progress is not an end in itself: an ideal state of justice enables people to autonomously make sense of the world – given the necessary social conditions. A philosophical anthropology can easily show that a 'will to truth' is an essential part of humanity. A humane society should do all it can to set people free to develop their talents and aptitudes.

Humanisation finally also means (c) to maximise happiness. Of course, we cannot guarantee that people will be happy, because happiness is not only a subjective feeling, but also something that must be accomplished individually. Happiness however denotes a 'will to completeness', a feeling of harmony with the whole of being that can be promoted by a general system of care and solidarity that starts with the care for oneself through one's own labour. This control of one's own life and this confidence in the support of others contributes significantly to the basic experience of happiness.

Getting specific

Specific research on humanisation has to focus on the dynamics of organisations and institutions from both a historical and a normative perspective. A theory of humanisation cannot be separated from what traditionally is called the history of mentality. A manager working in an organisation has to situate its actions in this historical and normative perspective. Like institutions, organisations also can be grouped together in subsystems of society. These subsystems are related to specific functions. Private bodyguard companies for instance belong to the general subsystem of security along with the army and the police, including also the Ministry of Defence and some parts of the Ministry of Justice.

With Vittorio Hösle (1997, p. 563–88) we may distinguish five basic subsystems or institutional domains of society: family, economy, military, religion and justice, with the first three guaranteeing biological necessities like reproduction, nutrition and security. The last two are dedicated to knowledge and behavioural coordination, which indirectly can also be linked to biological functions (since we need knowledge and coordination to survive). The state is intrinsically connected with the subsystems of security and justice but can envelop other subsystems, which have different autonomy depending on the type of society we are dealing with. I think we can link these institutional domains to the three basic paths of humanisation considered above.

The *family*, as I like to call the reproductive system of society, can be taken as the immediate expression of desire (love). Here the dominating discourse is and should be affective and expressive. The *economic* system can be traced back to the ability of living beings to partly control the world surrounding them. It is the first domain of power. The discourse dominating this domain is and should be based on righteousness and efficiency. Knowledge is intrinsically connected with the system of *religion* (and later science). Here the discourse is organised around terms like truth and wisdom. We can speak of a state when these three systems (of knowledge, power and love) are united by a system of security that provides protection from the outside, and by a system of justice protecting the inside.

The humanisation of these social systems heads towards a bifurcation of the 'idealism of dialogue' in specific types of organisations. On the level of state power humanisation is a process of democratisation going from an authoritarian structure based on fear to an open system of political participation. All the systems directly linked to the state, like justice and military, point in convergent directions. Justice is progressively transformed from a system based on prohibitions into a system based on fundamental rights (including rights of non-human beings). The state of law is still developing and expanding the domain of rights. The dynamics of the defence system goes from a military society to a highly (and finally totally) demilitarised society. The system of knowledge points to an 'epistemisation' of society. Religious, philosophical and scientific insights are made more and more accessible, extending their wings to an educational system based on the ideal of cognitive, moral and aesthetic formation (in German philosophy this is called Bildung). The economic system heads towards a *cooperative* system of labour in which material needs are strictly limited in terms of righteousness. The organisation of the economy will delineate a curve going from slavery, passing through competition, and ultimately arriving at a collaborative system envisioning the Common Good and mirroring dialogical reason.[6] Finally, the humanisation of society entails an extension of the system of care drawing a line from the cellular domain of the family to a system based on taking care of the planet. Humanity and nature are both becoming part of one large family.

Concluding remarks

To understand what the humanisation of organisations means, we need to understand the processes in which these organisations are involved. Each of these processes demands the specific attention of people within a managerial function. Humanisation of organisations constitutes a dynamic that heads towards the realisation of the 'idealism of dialogue' in the 'material structures' of society. For if we want to encourage humanisation on state level (from government to municipalities) we should develop different and new democratic structures rather than thinking that we have politically arrived at the end of history. Institutionalising democratic structures is a way to unfold the dialogical principle of equality. If we want to encourage humanisation on the level of organisations related to the idea of justice we should endeavour to extend the domain of rights to other than only human beings. If this is done, a dialogical attitude becomes the norm for more and more of our different relations. If we want to encourage humanisation on the level of the subsystem of defence we should encourage actions that make aggression and violence unnecessary. If we want to encourage humanisation on the level of knowledge we should develop broad ways of educational formation, including moral and aesthetic formation. If we want to encourage humanisation of the domain of the economy we should progressively abandon our system of competition in favour of a system based on cooperation. If we want to encourage the humanisation of the familiar domain we should extend the attitude of care to all other realms of society. Decisive changes need to take place inside the existing organisations of society. This urge to change our ways of living belongs to a profound moral imperative residing in us – an imperative of responsibility that will never cease to exhort and incite our actions.

Notes

1 I dedicate this Chapter to Prof. Douwe van Houten († 2010), founding father of the University of Humanistic Studies, whose work on humanisation gave me an everlasting impression of vivid human engagement.
2 It is in this sense that Douwe van Houten (2010) uses the term in his work.
3 I shall use the term 'ecology' instead of 'environment', because 'environment' implies that nature is a space surrounding humanity, whereas I would like to consider nature as having its own normative constitution.
4 The dialectics of Hegel seems to point in this direction (1969).
5 'I consider nothing animal to be strange to me!'
6 See *Humanisation of the Economy* in this volume.

References

Apel, K.O (1973) *Transformation der Philosophie. 2. Vol.* Frankfurt am Main: Suhrkamp.
Apel, K.O. and Kettner, M. (eds) (1992) *Zur Anwendung der Diskursethik in Politik, Recht und Wissenschaft.* Frankfurt am Main: Suhrkamp.
Bauer, J. (2008) *Das kooperative Gen. Abschied vom Darwinismus.* Hamburg: Hoffmann und Campe.
Blanchot, M. (1983) *La Communauté inavouable.* Paris: Minuit.
Böhler, D. (1992) *Diskursethik und Menschenwürdegrundsatz zwischen Idealisierung und Erfolgsverantwortung,* in: Apel, K.O. and Kettner, M. (eds) (1992) *Zur Anwendung der Diskursethik in Politik, Recht und Wissenschaft,* p. 201–31.
Brandom, R. (1994) *Making it explicit.* Boston: Harvard University Press.
Damasio, A. (2006) *Descartes' error. Emotion, reason, and the human brain.* London: Vintage.
Dewey, J. (2000) *Experience and nature.* New York: Dover.
Elias, N. (1976) *Über den Prozess der Zivilisation.* Frankfurt am Main: Suhrkamp.
Forst, R. (2007) *Das Recht auf Rechtfertigung.* Frankfurt am Main: Suhrkamp.
Foucault, M. (1984a) *L'Usage des plaisirs.* Paris: Gallimard.
Foucault, M. (1984b) *Le Souci de soi.* Paris: Gallimard.
Gadamer, H.G. (1990) *Wahrheit und Methode.* Tübingen: Mohr Siebeck.
Habermas, J. (1981) *Theorie des kommunikativen Handelns. 2. vol.* Frankfurt am Main: Suhrkamp.
Hegel, G.W.F. (1969) *Wissenschaft der Logik.* Frankfurt am Main: Suhrkamp.
Horkheimer, M. and Adorno, T. (1981) *Dialektik der Aufklärung.* Frankfurt am Main: Suhrkamp.
Hösle, V. (1997) *Moral und Politik. Grundlagen einer politischen Ethik für das 21. Jahrhundert.* München: Beck.
Jacobs, G. (ed.)(2008) *Goed werk. Verkenningen van normatieve professionalisering.* Amsterdam: SWP.
Jonas, H. (1997) *Die Entstehung der Werte.* Frankfurt am Main: Suhrkamp.

– (1992) *Das Prinzip Verantwortung*. Frankfurt am Main: Suhrkamp.
Kant, I. (1964) *Beantwortung der Frage: was ist Aufklärung?* Frankfurt am Main: Insel.
Leroi-Gourhan, A. (2006) *Les Religions de la préhistoire*. Paris: Puf.
– (1964). *Le Geste et la parole. Technique et langage*. Paris: Albin Michel.
Merleau-Ponty, M. (1945) *Phénoménologie de la perception*. Paris: Gallimard.
Morin, E. (2008) *La Méthode*. 6. vol. Paris: Seuil.
Popper, K. (1971) *The open society and its enemies, vol. 2: The high tide of prophecy: Hegel, Marx, and the aftermath*. Princeton: Princeton University Press.
Sarmiento, D.F. (2003) *Facundo. Civilización y barbarie* [Facundo. Civilisation and barbarism]. Buenos Aires: Stock Cero.
Taylor, C. (1989) *Sources of the self. The making of modern identity*. Boston: Harvard University Press.
van Houten, D. (2010) *Humanisering als uitdaging [Humanisation as challenge]*. Unpublished manuscript, Utrecht: University for Humanistic Studies.

2 Let's dance

On humanising and organisations

Ruud Kaulingfreks

Introduction

When we think about humanising we are at a loss. At face value it sounds very clear and valuable but asked to explain what we mean by it we have to admit it is very unclear. To make matters worse, humanising is an ideal. It is a concept we refer to often as something that should exist but is still not attained. Humanising is a normative concept and as such it holds a critique. The world is at present not humanised enough and we should make an effort for it. But what is it to humanise? How do we humanise? Or when? Then things get complicated since we do not have an answer ready at hand.

Especially when dealing with organisations humanising is seen as a must. Although the whole world should be humanised, organisations are the place where it is most needed. Organisations should be humanised! Sounds good and I've never encountered anyone who is against it. Who wants to dehumanise organisations? Or who does not want organisations to be humanised?

Humanising organisations

But what is humanising? Here we have a problem. We expect everyone to understand us and agree with us. Usually they do and nod so that the conversation can carry on about how to change organisations so that they become more humane. Then the troubles really start. Since we do not exactly know what humanising is, we are continually discussing ways of humanising. It is especially annoying when you boast to be able to humanise organisations. Organisations are used to having everything clear and well defined. In fact organisations are a domain where everything evolves around clear concepts and well-formulated intentions. Organisations are the domain of language, where people are constantly trying to act in accordance with predefined goals and means. Only when there is clarity, preferably measurable clarity, does the organisation act. In this sense organisations are extremely idealistic. They are driven by the idea (usually called policy). Experiences and reality itself are considered something that can be managed and controlled by ideas or concepts. Language comes in first; materiality follows language. Otherwise management would never give such an importance to, for instance, strategy, mission statement, vision, and the control of the market. Management, or the language of organisation, is full of concepts that create their own reality and become very real for the people in the organisation. Market is such a concept. One can only see the market once one believes in it. Organisations are very much about language and creating concepts that define the reality they exist in. Therefore the concepts have to be clear and specific so that there is no misunderstanding if the target (a word) has been attained and the performance indicators (another word) have been successfully reached.

Organisations cannot live with ambiguity or fuzzy concepts. They don't accept space for interpretation and diversity in meaning. Organisations and especially management are there to attain unity of means in order to deliver a specific output. That's one of the reasons for the love for figures. Seven is more than four, everybody knows that! Organisations don't like diversity or differences. The managerial ideal of an organisation is of a close team with no differences but shared values and opinions. In fact, the ideal is a permanent agreement on the firm and its achievements: 'We do the job together'. Protocols, policy, directives and mission statements are there to ensure that everyone knows the exact meaning of the language used and to ensure an agreement on the performance. It may sound harsh but organisations are a language game where the parole leads behaviour and where much attention is given to uniformity in beliefs and concepts. Language works here as a reality maker. Once the policy is expressed, it becomes a reality, guides the actions of all concerned and is seen in reality. People in the organisation perceive the policy in action as if it were real. They actually see the market, the clients, the share. Specific rules apply to who can speak in an organisation; who can sit at the table and discuss the decisions; and who forms parts of the selected group that creates the strategy and therefore the reality of the organisation, as was made clear by Barry and Elmers (1977), who state that strategy is a certain narrative that acquires a reality by the people that use it.

Ambiguity

If humanising has any chance of anchoring in organisations it should be clear and well defined and preferably made operational with *smart* indicators. Then it can be integrated in the language of organisations and become something everybody understands, and, more important, becomes attainable.

That's the problem with humanising. There is no unambiguous definition of it. No translation into practicality. Even more, we do not know exactly what it means. That is the purpose of this book. To make clear why humanising is important and to explain to the world what it is. So in a sense the lack of a proper description is a failure. We should be able to explain exactly what we mean by it and to make clear what is at stake when we talk about humanising organisations.

Or should we?

It is not my aim to clarify the concept and to give well-defined views on how to deal with humanising, nor to explain why humanising is badly needed. Others in this book can do that better than me. My interest is in the ambiguity, to make an apology of being at a loss. Not because I want to complicate things or because I'm intellectually lazy, but because I believe there is a value in not knowing, especially when dealing with organisations. The clarity and practicality organisations seek needs to be confronted with fuzziness and ambiguity. There is a value in not being specific and clear. The implicit has a place in our world, not only because we cannot be consciously aware of everything, or we just lack time to stop and think as Herbert Simons (1997) explained, but mainly because our mind is not totally in control of everything. The world is not a management project that can be made transparent according to our visions and policies. In our actions we continually deal with unknown quantities without much fuzz. We deal with things without first analysing them and acting according to a plan or strategy; we follow certain values because they feel right and just. When confronted with a breach of those values we feel ill at ease, sometimes physically unwell. It is Hubris to think that we can know everything and by that be in control, have the world in our hand. Nevertheless the assumption that organisations are an island of clearness in a fuzzy world is besides the truth. Organisations are very often fuzzy and thrive on it. Management very often makes decisions that can be interpreted in different ways and often are by the employees. Take mission statements as an example. Everybody agrees on them (or so they say) but often everybody has a different interpretation of what they stand for. Organisations are very seldom in agreement of what they do and act for. Still the language of organisations is full of attempts to make strategies and goals explicit and accountable. Smart statements (I mean the acronym SMART: Specific, Measurable, Assignable, Realistic, Time-related) are a value most organisations adhere to.

Mission statements

But maybe more important is that when things are clear and well defined we tend to forget about them. Once something is known we don't think about it. What everyone knows is not worth thinking, and becomes superfluous. Once known, something is put outside discussions and we don't search anymore. It becomes an asset as if it were an object that the more we use the less we see. It is just useful and we forget about it.

It is a little like the mission statements of most firms. They are created to make the purpose of the firm clear to everybody. The making of such a statement is usually an intense process with a lot of discussion because it touches the core of the firm. It expresses what the firm is and what its purpose is. Because it needs to express what is common to everyone it usually is a complicated sentence that says too much in a short space. Once it is agreed upon it usually is printed on a card and distributed to everyone. In the beginning it is shown and repeated everywhere and sometimes discussed. After a while however it becomes something that nobody cares about and disappears in drawers. Only when somebody from the outside comes and asks about it do people explain it and that is it. Nobody remembers exactly what it is about but everyone remembers the discussions when it was created. Nobody speaks again of the purpose or the mission of the firm. Referring to the printed mission statement in meetings silences the discussion. In other words nobody thinks about it anymore and as said everyone has, despite the long discussion, a different interpretation of it.

The more we know something the less we reflect upon it and the less meaning it has. Known things lose their shine and become meaningless, like a tool in the garage. It is like Jean Baudrillard said: 'When with the aid of a computer we know all the names of God, the world ends and the stars stop shining' (1990, p. 140).

Docta Ignorantia

It is not my intention to advocate for lack of knowledge or intellectual laziness. We need to think and the result of thinking is understanding. That is saved in knowledge. Without understanding, the world is unliveable and we are at the mercy of demons. Because we understand we can have some grip on the world and we can act. What I want to put forth is a praise of a thinking that is conscious of its tentative character and knows that it does not know enough, a thinking that is driven by the awareness of partiality: knowing that we don't know. No matter how much we know there always will be an unthinkable rest that we cannot reach. There always will be aporias as Derrida continually repeated and reminded (1994). We need to think in the line of Cusanus' *De Docta Ignorantia* (2007).

According to him the more we think, the more aware we are that there is a lot that we don't know. When we start to think about something we do not have an overview of the field and do not know what it is all about. The more we get into something the more we understand that we are just at the beginning and that we don't know much about it. This sense of not knowing enough only gets bigger the more we dig into it. We become aware of what we still need to know or in other words we are intensely aware of our lack of knowledge. This is especially so with big subjects and Cusanus is of course talking about God, the infinitely big and therefore the subject we will never know. The bigger the subject the more aware we are of our lack of knowledge. Hence *docta ignorantia* or learned ignorance.

Science does not annihilate the *docta ignorantia* but is directed to make us aware of our lack and therefore invites us to think further. A science accentuates that the world is always larger than our knowledge and we always are on the way to knowledge. Thinking is being aware of this lack and knowing we never will surpass it. As Heidegger said it is a thankful thinking (*dankend denken*) (1970, p. 51).

This is of special importance when dealing with sense. Meaning always escapes us in the sense that when we articulate it, it loses its meaning. By naming it, sense becomes senseless. It becomes the name and sense is veiled. Of course we name it because putting it to words unveils the sense. There is always the double movement of veiling and unveiling, as Heidegger explained masterly throughout his work.

Sense

Sense is always related to questions and not to answers. Sense drives us to ask further and is seldom satisfied with answers. Sense is more a drive than the answer itself. It is because of sense that we ask questions, often not even about the sense itself. It is a search for meaningfulness that drives us to pose questions and to search for knowledge. Sense is aligned to a lack; there is always the desire to make sense, to reach a meaningful situation. This is not to say that we always are discontent. Even in a meaningful situation we can continue our search for meaning. Sense is never done and ready but it always is ahead of us, despite the common assumption enclosed in the expression, 'that makes sense'. 'That makes sense' is used to denote agreement. Somebody says something that makes us think and we agree with it; it makes sense. But this does not mean the sense is articulate. This is meaningful but the moment I realise that, I start searching for it otherwise it becomes senseless. It loses its meaning the moment I define it as meaningful. There is a difference between thinking of something and thinking from something. The latter is a driving force that pushes thinking in a certain direction. The former is the object of thinking and becomes analysis. One can think about care, for instance, and analyse and construct opinions about it. But one can also think from care. The subject can be something completely different but is imbued in the caring thoughts.

Intuition

Analysis presupposes a distance between the subject and the object. We study and analyse something always from the outside as something alien. It presupposes language and concepts. Thinking from sense is, on the other hand, thinking from within and is led by sympathy. This is sense thinking. It is a thinking that is led by attention to the object, that is, one opens up to the object and lets it speak without pinning it down beforehand in a conceptual framework. What appears is sense and this leads and pushes thinking and comprehension forward.

Bergson makes a well-known difference between analyses and intuition that helps to clarify this point. Analyses or intellectual knowledge is always from outside the object and is dependent on the perspective one takes and the concepts one uses. It explains by putting the object in relation with other known objects. It depends on the rules of language. In a famous analogy he explains: 'All the pictures of a city, taken from all possible perspectives could complete each other very well, but they always fall short to the three dimensional city one strolls through' (1959, p. 1394). Intuition is always knowledge from within the object and is not dependent on concepts or perspectives. One becomes the object in sympathy. But intuition has no language; it is mute and cannot be expressed in concepts. There is no language for intuitions. It manifests itself as vague haze around the intellect and has a power of negation. Intuition lets us know when something is not right, it doesn't feel good, it makes us uneasy. Intuition steers intellect, it colours and drives the intellectual quest without making it clear what it is we search for. But it is clearly present when we stumble upon something, or makes us continue our search because we are not content with what we have got. Intuition is thinking from within and needs the concepts of the intellect to come to the fore. But every concept falls short in expressing the intuition. There is always more that continues nagging. Philosophy is according to Bergson nothing more than a search for the right concepts, to create concepts that correspond to the intuition (Bergson, 1959, p. 1347). But we never succeed. Knowledge remains implicit although we all have a perfect sense of what it is all about. There is a continuous friction between explicit knowledge in concepts and the speechless but pushy intuition. As Nietzsche said: 'we stand still in front of intuition, owe stutter or talk in forbidden metaphors and unheard combination of concepts' (1967, p. 889). Or as Barthes put it in *La Leçon* we can only express it by cheating with language (1978, p. 20). Sense cannot be put into words, but words express meaning; they refer to sense. Referring to means that the sense is not in the words themselves but outside them. As de Saussure (2013) made very clear the signifier is not the same as the signified; the word dog is not a dog and does not bite. It only denotes the actual animal. Sense is evoked by language but escapes the concepts. To think that sense is in language is according to Barthes a fatal alienation (1978, p. 16). And to make matters worse he added that we cannot escape it. Language is a *huit clos*. Sense is not in the language itself but language makes sense. It refers to sense; otherwise it is pointless. Sense can only be expressed, or express itself in language. The alienation comes because in order to express sense we are forced to adapt to the rules of language. Language forces us to speak in a given manner and forces us to speak only in the way language accepts. Barthes concludes that language is just fascism since fascism is not the prohibition of speaking but the obligation to speak (1978, p. 18).

Presentational thinking

Another thinker that warned against a trust in language and concepts is Susan Langer. According to her language distorts reality by transforming the meaning into the rules of language:

> [A]ll language has a form which requires us to string out our ideas even though their objects rest one within the other; as pieces of clothing that are actually worn one over the other have to be strung side by side on the clothesline … only thoughts which can be arranged in this peculiar order can be spoken at all; any idea which does not lend itself to this 'projection' is ineffable, incommunicable by means of words.' (1942, p. 81)

This property she calls discursiveness. But we are not entirely doomed; beside discursiveness there is another modus that precedes it. That is presentativeness. The presentational form is the recognition of sensible patterns in perception that lead to the creation of words and language. In order to have a discursive form a certain activity needs to be done beforehand. We create words that have meaning, that say something. This creation cannot be discursive since it distorts meaning. So there is a pre language activity that creates language. This activity is by no means irrational. The poet is painfully aware he is creating poetry, the artist knows and calculates very precisely where and how to paint. However they are not relying on the existing discourse since they are creating or transforming sense into a form. As Bergson said they are driven by knowledge from within the object, they are driven by intuition (Bergson, 1959, p. 495, 497).

Presentation is for Langer a form of thinking that is not driven by *discoursiveness* but creates discourse. It speaks by creating or, almost as Nietzsche said, in unheard and unknown combination of concepts (1967, p. 889, see above). In other words, it cheats and does not stick to the rules.

Rest

Trusting in definitions and searching well-defined descriptions of concepts distorts reality and misleads us by making us think the language reality coincides with the world. Putting trust into words creates an *ersatz* world of words that responds only to itself and not to reality. It creates a discursive world that in the end proves to be meaningless and veils meaning. Policy becomes a reality in itself and creates its reality dis-attached from the experienced world. We end up seeing a 'market' or believing in the need for strategy and market domination. Or we end up believing that we know exactly what humanising is and creating a step-by-step plan to achieve it. Or worse creating a humanising scan and benchmark …

I believe humanising is too important an idea to be pinned down in a discourse and to be conceptually clear. It is a sense-making idea anchored in a moral intuition or desire to transform the world into a more humane place. This is especially true in organisations since they put too much emphasis on efficiency and competitive advantage and often forget about the people involved. As long as the idea remains fuzzy there is space for discussion and thinking. Humanising appeals to a vague sentiment that nevertheless manifests itself very strongly in a moral indignation and a political desire to better the world. Humanising is a presentative idea that appeals as a value to be pursued and is open for discussion, and reflection. It is an aspiration that inspires one to search, but brings us together in the recognition of a joint effort. As long as we talk about humanisation we encounter others engaged in the same aspiration (I will not say quest in order not to dramatise it to much).

This does by no means mean we should not talk about humanising. We are language driven and we search continually for clarification. We cannot accept fuzziness as a permanent state of affairs. But we have to be very aware that each possible articulation of sense immediately veils it and that the big danger lies in believing our words. There always is a rest that escapes us. This rest is the place of sense. We need to be aware of this rest in all our thinking. We need to think from a respect for what escapes us. As said, it is *hubris* to think that we can know everything. We could end up like Faust.

Weak thinking

So, what am I aiming at? When we deal with sense making we deal with an ethos, a direction that defines our actions and judgements. Ethos speaks of vagueness, of a fuzzy direction that still pushes us by telling what is right or wrong. An ethos is behind our words and gives them meaning, directs our speech without being part of it; it makes us think from it, not about it. It makes us continually search for sense, for a right articulation. The emphasis is on the search, not on the finding. As long as we search we are painfully aware we haven't found it. We know we are searching and we haven't got it, a little bit like when we lose our keys. We know they are here somewhere and the more we search the more we are aware they must be somewhere and we don't have them. We cannot forget about them because they dominate our thought. We have to find them and we must continue our search.

The search for meaning is a creation that produces new concepts and new knowledge as a stepping-stone for further searching. In a sense it is stretching the value of stuttering, of being at a loss and searching for words. Or, on the other hand, it is a critique of clarity and complacency with well-defined definitions and policies. A critique of shared concepts and management advise.

Searching for words and fuzziness invites conversation. We do not search on our own but we share it with others. Morality, ethos, sense are never individual matters but they form community. We share the search and even the embarrassment of not being clear, of stuttering. In this sense humanising belongs to what Vattimo called weak thinking (2013), thinking that is very aware of its lack of claims to reality. Thinking that is aware of the difference between its discursiveness and the world itself. It cannot claim truth or hard evidence for its claims and does not pass the tentativeness of a search for words, does not surpass the vagueness of the search and is therefore weak. In this sense humanising creates a shared search and makes us recognise others engaged in the embarrassment of not being able (or refusing) to be specific and accountable.

Conversations and meetings

Because it is weak we need to share it in a conversation. It is implicit and tacit knowledge, as said; therefore we search with others based on the same ethos. We have a conversation where the differences are explored and compared: maybe we mean more or less the same. Conversations never end; they just stop in order to continue some other time. We need more conversations in organisations, even if we lose time with them. Conversations make sense; they let meaning emerge in between the words. A conversation is a free interchange of ideas and a common search for meaning. It is held without other aim than the sharing and the interchange. Conversations are abundant and there is never a shortage. They are esthetical in the sense that they are held for the pleasure of the conversation itself, not with the explicit goal of reaching agreement. They are a friction or encounter of ideas and tentative formulations fed with the words of the other. Conversations hold communities together; they are the communal activity par excellence and by engaging in conversations we participate in the same community of searchers. We share a common experience that maybe transforms into actions but not necessarily so. It suffices that we share and that sense emerges. Conversations inspire; that in itself is enough. The rest is management.

A conversation is essentially different from a meeting. A meeting is negotiations and trying to win. It is directed to reach consensus on a decision that is supported by all. In a meeting there are parties engaged in a discussion about who will have his or her standpoint accepted. A meeting is always antagonistic and everyone comes well prepared and with clear views. The goal is to overcome the differences, not to support them.

A meeting is all about calculations and winning, it is about presenting your own views in a well-spoken manner and convincingly. A meeting is about making things explicit in decisions that stand out and work. There is no weak thinking in meetings, but convictions and positions to defend. A meeting is an adequate way of communication among management and teams in organisations. The PowerPoint logic of bullets convince easier than long discourses. One cannot be at a loss for words in a meeting. In sum, it is the opposite of a conversation or sharing.

Implicit knowledge, or not knowing, has a great value. When it comes to sense making then it is even important not to rely on the conceptual articulation but to keep it open. Concepts and discursive thinking closes the possibilities of meaning by veiling it and creating a language reality that gives a sense of knowing and control, therefore weakening the meaning. It looks like we have grasped meaning and we do not reflect anymore. When everything is known the stars stop shining and we enter a world of technical calculations where control reigns, but devoid of sense. Everything is at hand and the only concern becomes the right way to manage and control the world.

My plea is for a permanent conversation about humanising corporations and the world at large in a shared search for what is human and what we need to do in order to make organisations care about humanity and the people involved. We cannot know exactly what we mean by it but we need to talk about it, to search and develop the ethos of humanising. It may sound paradoxical but although we never found the right words for sense, the vehicle for sense making is language. We cannot put it into words but we need to keep trying and keep talking about it.

Sensibility

Humanising is meaningful as an ethos, tacit knowledge that steers our search for meaning. Humanising is more related to sensibility than to conceptual clarification, sensibility that opens us to something that we don't know but nevertheless is there and, as a vague haze, makes us act and think in a certain direction. Humanising is more about the intensity of the tone than the music itself: '*C'est le ton qui fait la musique*' as the old adagio says. Humanising points out to a sensibility from where we talk, a care for values and people before intellectual clarity or good management. Sensibility however does not exist in itself but needs a language that preserves it and evokes it, that reminds us that an ethos is constantly needed and that we have to be faithful to it. In this sense sensibility is profoundly moral and for that matter political. Weak thinking is a political stance that opposes the clarity and certainty of the already known and reminds us that we do not control the world and that not everything is in our hands. There is much to aspire for, even if it is utterly unclear what that exactly is. Humanising is a moral and political sensibility that makes us look further and search for ways to change the world into a more humane place whatever that may be. In conversations and shared research we may understand it better but let's hope we never reach the point where we can define it and think we know what it precisely is. It is a political position to confront organisations with our stuttering and not give the answer they expect when it comes to humanising. It is important to demonstrate the ethos of it, the sensibility of a weak thinking that nevertheless is strong enough to claim a spot in the world. That even claims it is much needed, especially in organisations.

References

Barry, D. and Elmers, M. (1977) 'Strategy retold: Towards a narrative view of strategic discourse', *Academy of Management Review* 22 (2), p. 429–52.
Barthes, R. (1978) *La Leçon*. Paris: Seuil.
Baudrillard, J. (1990) *Fatal Strategies*, Los Angeles: Semiotext(e).
Baudrillard, J. (2001) *De fatale strategieen* [Les Strategies Fatales] (Nio, M. trans.). Amsterdam: De Vrije Uitgevers.
Bergson, H. (1959) *Oevres*. Paris: PUF Edition du Centenaire.
Cusanus, N. (2007) *De docta ignorantia* [Of learned ignorance]. Eugene, OR: Wipf and Stock Publisher.
de Saussure, F. (2013) *Course in general Linguistics*. London: Bloomsbury Academic Reprint.
Derrida, J. (1994) *Aporias*. New York: Stanford University Press.
Heidegger, M. (1970) *Wat is metafysica?* (trans. van Nierop, M.). Utrecht Tielt: Lannoo.
Heidegger, M. (1978) What is metaphysics? In: *Basic writings*. London: Routledge.
Heidegger, M. (2009) *Wat is Metafysica?* [Was ist Metaphysik?] (Klostermann, V. trans.). Utrecht Tielt: Lannoo.
Langer, S. (1942) *Philosophy in a new key: A study in the symbolism of reason, rite and art*. Cambridge, MA: Harvard University Press.
Nietzsche, F. (1967) *Kritische Studienasugabe Herausgegeben von Giorgio Colli und Mazzino Montinari. Band 1: Ueber Waarheit und Luge im aussermoralischen Sinne*. Berlin: de Gruyter.
Simons, H. (1997) *Administrative behaviour*. New York: Free Press.
Vattimo, G. (2013) *Weak thought*. New York: State University of New York Press.

3 A sense of consultancy

The humanising effort of problematisation

Martijn Simons

Introduction

After the prosperity of consultancy in the 1990s and early 2000s, the booming days of consultancy are behind us. The unclear and cluttered field of consultancy has become a jungle of companies providing advice from every area of expertise. Use Google (one of the most used and commonly known consultants of our time) and you will find IT Consultancy, Creative Consultancy, Employment Consultancy, Management Consultancy, Process Consultancy, Elevator Consultancy, Educational Consultancy and Magic Consultancy. Gilbert Toppin and Fiona Czerniawaska (2005) even consult the field of consultancy by explaining why and how the field of consultancy should change.

All these different consultants have one thing in common. Their focus is on the knowledge and experience used to help the customer or client to solve a problem at hand in order to improve processes, organisations etc. Consultants use knowledge, experience and skills to fix problems. The logic of this systematic, instrumental and impersonal problem solving is most commonly known as the expert logic of consultancy.

This outside-in consultancy is useful when, for instance, my computer or my bicycle breaks down, or when I have a toothache. But the same logic is used for more complex, social and interpersonal problems. The instrumental and impersonal approach of the expert logic has proven to be of little help here. From the attempt at efficient and systematic problem solving, so-called *wicked problems* result: problems resulting from solving problems.

The issue here is that the problem does not carry the same logic as the solution. While the problem is social, interpersonal, complex, moral and human, the solution is analytic, instrumental, systematic, and above all impersonal. This puzzle does not fit. Complex interpersonal problems ask for a vital and dialogical approach. Often, instrumental and single-minded problem solving mutes the humanising voice of the social and dialogical. With a focus on solving problems, consultancy lacks the attention for the problem itself and the social usefulness and humanising effect of problematisation. This humanising effect can be derived from the core and roots of consultancy, *consultare*: to discuss.

This chapter will argue that problems are worth problematising. Problematisation is valuable in organisations in terms of learning processes and interpersonal relations. Therefore problems are very important for consultancy and humanisation in organisations. The central question in this article is: *How can consultants use an effective humanising approach to help organisations to engage with problems?*

The process of problematisation moves from an outside-in logic of problem solving towards an inside-out emerging of knowledge from the problem itself. The focus moves from technical managerial expert knowledge to the humanising value of dialogue, sense making and the interpersonal emergence of knowledge through problematisation.

A dialogical process that contributes to what Kaulingfreks calls *the creation of human value within the organisation*,[1] born from (moral) sensibility and discussion in search of humanisation. We no more believe our words and trust the answers, than start asking questions, listen and enter into open dialogue beyond goals and targets. The process of problematisation has become a search for meaning and sense in organisations.

The search of this chapter starts at an abstract level with social and philosophical theories advocating problematisation as a vital process in organisations. These theories focus on interactive learning and emerging knowledge through problematisation. From this abstract level we move to practices in which inexperienced young professionals are confronted with organisational social issues. Their lack of experience, the questions they raise and their openness towards the issue are valuable as an intervention born from doing justice to the problem at hand.

Problem solving

Since the introduction of scientific management by Frederick Taylor in the early 1900s, science and management have been closely intertwined. In the introduction of *The Principles of Scientific Management* (1911) Taylor points out three main goals of his book. He wants to show that inefficiency is a problem from which organisations are suffering, that systematic management is a remedy for this inefficiency, and that management is a true science. This direct link between science and management leads to an approach in which organisational processes rest upon laws, rules and principles that can be rationally analysed and improved. In scientific management, also known as Taylorism, the efficiency of organisational processes is a rational mechanism that can be adjusted by measuring and reconstructing the process in order to get objective production standards. Organisational processes become assembly lines, a system of standardisation, synchronisation and specialisation serving production. The first management consultancies therefore were by nature very analytical and technical.

Although a lot has changed since the introduction of scientific management, the core ideas of efficiency and the focus on rationality, measurement and instrumentality still stands strong. The consequence of this focus is that the process of organisation as an interpersonal and human activity is highly undervalued. Even new popular management consultancy methods that are supposed to be dialogical and human centred, such as 'lean' and 'lean six sigma', are highly affected by the analytical and instrumental approach to organisational processes and scientific management. Although 'lean' appears to focus on the involvement of employees, this involvement has a highly instrumental character. The main goal of lean processes is to solve a problem by reducing waste and by continuous improvement of the process. The highest state of organisation processes is flow that can be reached by discovering defects and errors and removing them in order to reduce variations in the organisational process. De facto there are not so many differences between Taylor's assembly line and the flow in the 'lean'[2] approach. Problems are a hiccup in the flow or the assembly line, which can be overcome by analysing the problem, measuring and quantifying it (for instance the hours spent and the amount of manual actions) and repairing the defects and errors.

When organisational problems are most of all regarded as technical hiccups in organisational processes, it means that consultancy solves organisational problems by overcoming these technical hiccups. This means that a consultant is first and foremost an expert who knows how to fix a certain organisational problem. The consultant appears to be no part of the organisational process; she or he only has to know the problem. The consultant analyses, measures and repairs the problem. Solving an organisational problem is quite often regarded as an objective and instrumental intervention, which I characterise as expert logic. In this logic, solving organisational problems is an activity on the same level as the repair of my computer or solving a toothache. Consultancy, with its preoccupation with the objective and the instrumental that derives from efficient and systematic problem solving, reduces problems that are vital, complex and interpersonal in organisations. However, this instrumental and impersonal approach has proven to be of little help, for instance because new problems result from solving problems by reducing the complexity of the problem (Churchman, 1967; Rittel and Webber, 1973), because the logic of the solution does not fit the logic of the problem (Nohria and Beer, 2000) or because social problems are not always logic and discursive (Chia, 1996) but also existential and ethical (Kunneman, 2005).

Social and human interactions in organisations are an important part of organisational processes but are highly undervalued in consultancy. Social interaction in organisations is mostly regarded as the soft side and is only of value as a means toward an end. Human interactions are cogs in a large piece of machinery that can be set and repaired. We see this line of thought in 'lean' consultancy in which human interaction is reduced to time spent or movements made in the organisation process. The employees involved are mainly seen as experts who know how many movements must be made in order for normal processes to work or in order to function as part of the support for implementation.

In one of my last years in college I encountered consultants with such an expert approach. In those years I had a part-time job as a receptionist for about eight to ten hours per week in a fairly small academic institution. I liked my job because I encountered very different people, learned something about the organisation I worked for, and tried to be of service where and whenever I could. In the context of a large reorganisation within this organisation, I received a form with a chart of all my activities: receiving e-mail, answering e-mail, opening the door, making calls, receiving people etc. The question of the consultant, which I never saw in person, was if I could express all my activities in hours spent and full-time equivalent. I became a full-time equivalent (fte), what I did became fte. The value of my job was reduced to a number. As a student in critical organisations and intervention studies, learning a lot about humanisation in organisations and human dignity in organisations, I refused to be a cog in the machine.

Of course it is important to note that technical solutions are a perfect fit for technical problems. But reducing complex social interaction – and most social issues in organisations are far beyond making calls and receiving people – to a problem that can be solved by impersonal, instrumental and technical means, only leads to new problems. These are so-called *wicked problems*: problems resulting from solving problems. The main issue here is that the problem does not carry the same logic as the solution. While the problem is social, interpersonal, complex, moral and human, the solution is analytic, instrumental, systematic, and above all impersonal. With a focus on instrumentally solving the problem, expert consultancy lacks the attention for the problem itself and the social and humanising effect of problematisation. This humanising effect can be derived from the core and roots of consultancy, *consultare*: to discuss.

Problematisation

In order to get to an approach to consultancy and problem solving that has eye for humanisation in organisations, we have to prioritise the social aspect of problems in organisations and the way it can foster knowledge that helps to solve an organisational problem from the inside out. A humanising perspective on problem solving reflects the social problems in organisations. Management theory in general lacks an adequate discussion of these social problems. By gathering sensible and social concepts, a focus on humanisation gives us new concepts, insights and skills in order to discover the nature of social problems in organisations.

Therefore we have to respect what I call problematisation in organisations. Instead of jumping into solutions, most problems are worth problematising because of the learning processes, emerging knowledge and interpersonal relations involved. This makes problematisation one of the most humanising activities in organisations. To get a better understanding of problematisation in organisations, we have to get to what Burrell calls 'the absent centre of management theory': philosophy[3] (Burrell, 1989). Usually, philosophy is associated with abstract ideas, difficult books and bearded old men. While this is all too true, philosophy can also be concrete and practical in its application which helps us to rethink and reanimate organisational practices. One of the most inspiring philosophers to rethink our everyday life in organisations is the philosophy of Gilles Deleuze (1925–1995). With his focus on ongoing events of relational processes, he makes way for vital perspectives on social interactions in organisations.[4] An intensification of the attention for vital perspectives on social interactions can be seen in Deleuzian interpretations in organisation and social studies. The Deleuzian focus on the innovative and *interplex* processes of organisation are extensively discussed by organisation theorists like Stephen Linstead, Michael Pedersen and Bent Meier Sørensen.

Instead of regarding organisations as a mechanical and technical system, Deleuzian philosophy regards organisations as continuous creative and relational flows in which the *elan vital* of organisations is emphasised. Organisations continuously change in everyday practices. Although organisational processes are quite often seen as a repetition of work, as Ford did when he regarded organisational processes as an assembly line, organisational processes actually get shaped in the way people 'reply to each other' (cf. Linstead, 2002, p. 95 and further). The actualisation of organisational processes emerges from a composition of new and repetitive actions (cf. Deleuze 2004; 2004a; 2004b). Organisational processes are what Deleuze calls assemblages[5] of the repetitive plane of organisation (the world as we know it) through planes of immanence (an intensively dynamic state) towards new planes of organisational processes. These continuous dynamics between repetition and change are the creative forces of the organisation.[6]

One of the events in which we can see this vital process is problematisation. That is in not trying to solve it but to stay in the problem, to discuss it, to live it through. In more philosophical terms:

> [T]o push the problem towards a liminal crisis between a deterritorialization and possible reterritorializations, that is, to push it into a critical passage. Organisation theory should be exactly that: an elaborately developed question, rather than a resolution to a problem, an elaboration to the very end, of the necessary implications of a formulated question. … It is time for you to enter into your crisis and find a problem worth problematising.' (Sørensen, 2005, p.131) (cf. Fuglsang and Sørensen, in: Fuglsang and Sørensen (eds.), 2006, p. 16).

Digging deeper into the problem at hand entails a deeper understanding of the situation from which knowledge and solutions emerge and can be discussed. Instead of finding an external body of knowledge in the expert logic, solving problems emerges from the interpersonal logic of sense and dialogue. Instead of detaching ourselves from the problem by solving[7] it from outside-in, it is more important to relate to the problem at hand. Instead of saving time and solving a problem, we have to take time to live the problem. In contrast to what lean methodology wants us to believe, we have to waste time to solve problems, because organising takes time.

Taking time and solving problems

One of the main characteristics of problematisation is that we have to take our time to relate to the problematic situation at hand. It is what philosopher Henri Bergson[8] describes as an intuitive process or a process of intellectual sympathy. Intellectual sympathy starts from the idea that there is a direct, strong and vital relation between human beings and their contextual setting. The starting point in the relation is contact with progress, which Bergson calls duration. This is the qualitative and direct relation we have to the processes of everyday life (for instance in organisations). In Bergson's philosophy taking time for human interaction is most important for knowledge creation, because knowledge about (organisational) progress emerges from progress itself (cf. Linstead, S. and Mullarkey, J. [2003]). Knowledge born from progress itself produces custom-made knowledge instead of general, ready-made understanding of the world. Knowledge is not static, but vital, changeful and creative in its application. Knowledge is not something that exists detached from reality, but is deeply intertwined with life. (cf. Styhre, 2003[9], 2004)[10].

With regard to outside-in problem solving in organisations, this means that the analytical, scientific knowledge about how an organisation should work takes precedence over everyday life in organisations. Bergson calls this instrumental and mechanic approach to everyday life the *cinematographic tendency* of the intellect. Our intellectual capacity enables us to approach reality *as if* it is a chain of immobile moments or parts representing the continuity of life through time *(duration)* (Bergson, 1998, 2001, 2004). We can see this for instance in protocols which are not everyday life in organisation but pretend to represent and dictate life in organisations. Nurses *know* what they have to do in which amount of time; they know which steps they have to take to care before they even have seen a patient. If I have problems with the behaviour of my colleague, complaining or solving the problem is organised in different steps of the protocol. This kind of cinematographic organisation of everyday life in organisations detaches us from the actual experience of taking care or being upset with someone. If we want to understand what it is to take care, to be upset or to solve organisational problems, we should do more justice to everyday vital, practical and professional knowledge in organisations.[11] To understand life in organisations a vital professional knowing is needed that sympathises with ongoing reality that creates an ordination of knowledge. It is knowledge that continuously organises itself from the inside out, it is continuous knowledge in progress that is both change and repetition. It becomes a continuous creative act of affirmation and discussion of existing protocols and ordination of knowledge. This challenges the expert approach of problem solving in organisations. The obviousness of intellectual and scientific knowledge is put at stake in a Bergsonian approach.[12] Scientific truth claims about organisational processes are challenged by sympathetic knowledge in organisations.

This means that problem solving through problematisation demands direct contact with the problem as a living reality (*elan vital*). In problematisation, people involve themselves in the joint venture of the organisational problem *and* they are involved with each other. This means that problematisation is a continuous creative process in which solving a problem is an emergent, spontaneous and relational activity. Solving problems emerges from everyday life in organisations as different sympathetic relations. Intellectual sympathy therefore indicates a living ethical and personal relation of connectedness in diversity. This is a perspective that has a better connection with social problems in organisation and shows characteristics of humanisation as part of problem solving in organisations.

A sense of consultancy

After showing the dehumanising effects of the mechanical outside-in approach of expert consultancy, and considering the interpersonal involvement with the organisational process the real expertise, the question arises if there is any room left for consultancy. Does consultancy still make sense? It does. As long as it has a sense of *consultare*: discussion, personal interaction and making organisations sensitive to what is happening and at stake. This means that the consultant is conscious of the core of his own work, to discuss, and the consultant as a person comes into play. Consultancy, then, becomes a personal attitude stimulating problem solving instead of being the one to solve the problem. In order to discuss organisational problems consultancy is born from using senses and questioning common sense. It does not start with pre-existing ideas and models as a solution, but arrives at them. For consultancy to make sense, it has to unfold knowledge.

I received a better understanding of this kind of consultancy, paradoxically, from young professionals who are not (yet) consultants, working on a project called *Kickstart your Social Impact*.[13] In this project we help highly educated young professionals who can't find a job directly after college. In interdisciplinary teams they work as starting consultants with complex organisational problems. We coach and train the young professionals to cope with this new experience of working in an organisation and working as a consultant.

What I noticed while coaching these teams was that it doesn't help the organisations much to make a model to solve the problem, create a comprehensive project plan or write reports with the 'right' answer to the problem at hand that tells them what they have to do to solve the problem. Most of these young professionals have never even used management models to solve problems nor written a comprehensive project plan for organisational problem solving. They actually *don't know* the answers to organisational problems, and they do not have the experience yet.

What they *can* do, and what helps the organisations most, is talking and listening to people and asking 'stupid' but critical questions, using their (common) sense to discover the problem at hand or to discover the interests of different stakeholders. They are naïve, intuitive and sympathetic in their interpersonal approach. Emerging from this curious and wondering attitude is a process of problematisation. Key to this emerging problematisation are their intended or unintended critical questions and actions. *Because* they are not part of the organisation, *because* they are not experts, but because they relate to the problem at hand, they create new insights, narratives and ways of working from which new knowledge and action unfolds. In this sense, consultancy becomes an attitude of curiosity and interest, of knowing and questioning which is very different from the attitude of the expert-consultant that has knowledge ahead of time and answers in advance.

One of the teams of young professionals worked on a project at one of the largest banks in the Netherlands. The central question they worked with was how the bank could get customers with a mortgage at the bank interested in sustainability, for instance in solar collectors or improving isolation. Talking with different stakeholders, the team discovered that the decision makers at the bank thought it was useful to aim at sustainability but didn't know exactly why. Throughout the organisation there were very different perspectives on what sustainability means. They gathered all the decision makers and started a dialogue with them about *their* perspectives on sustainability and *their* ideas about the importance of the subject. By asking why they think it is important, they figured out how to translate it into effective and appropriate messages to their customers. During the evaluation of the project, one of the decision makers told me that it was a 'risk' to work with inexperienced young professionals because they don't know how the organisation works etc. But it was this same 'risk' of which he spoke that had brought him the best insights and had delivered the most results for the project. The 'consultants' had helped to unfold these insights because of their fundamental questions and it was because of their talking with people apart from their position within the organisation that they were as effective as they were inexperienced.

Other examples were the *reception experience project* and consulting a professional sports club that wanted to help youngsters suffering from a lack of exercise. The team working on the reception experience project observed the interactions and talked to different employees of the organisation and users of the building, but most of all they used themselves as tools of experience. What happens when I step out of the bus and can't find the building while it's right in front of me? What bothers me most? By observing, talking and using their own experience, the team started to undertake actions to improve the reception experience.

The sports club had sport fields available for youngsters that are suffering from a lack of exercise. Talking to the youngsters and the organisation, the team discovered first of all that the youngsters didn't see themselves as 'suffering' from a lack of exercise. Secondly it appeared the fields were only available for use during school hours. After school members of the sports club occupy all fields. Common sense was applied here, and it led the team back to the organisation to talk about a more a positive approach to the youngsters, for example by stimulating a healthy lifestyle, and to consider cooperating with schools on this project because the schools can gather and mobilise the youngsters at times when the sports fields are available. The sports club simply had not considered this option before. By using their senses and their common sense these teams of young professionals stimulated new perspectives and solutions emerging from vital interaction with the organisation and stakeholders.

By living consultancy, these young professionals are searching for living knowledge and living solutions that are often both simple and effective. By being the 'Socrates' of the organisational problem they pass the 'common sense' of the organisation to get to a para-sense[14] of the problem by problematising the known and the self-evident. They innovate from interpersonal relations and by stimulating new interpersonal relations. They discuss or stimulate discussions like true consultants and (co-)create solutions nobody, including themselves, expected at first.

The humanising effort of consultancy

Now, what can we learn from the young professionals that live consultancy? In the examples we see that different stakeholders open up to learn from the problem at hand. The profession of consultancy consists of creating and stimulating a sensibility for problems by opening up a dialogue and asking questions. In this process of questioning and discussing, different stakeholders gather around the problem at hand. From this process of problematisation, the reflective turn emerges from experience and discovers[15] both problem and solution.

The humanising effort of a consultant is to be in touch with the problem at hand, and have a feeling for it and the people involved. By intuitively asking questions an open dialogue emerges from which different standpoints and personal relations to the problem evolve. In discovering the problem, solutions are not put forward as forms of expert knowledge by consultants. In the encounter, a multiverse is created around the problem[16] of which all stakeholders are trying to make sense. The interacting universes with their own sets of rules and ways are stimulated and become confused and reorganised by the confrontation. From this 'trembling' experience of not knowing, reflection, and searching for new ways to relate to the problem, new insights emerge as lines of flight.[17]

Instead of solving problems, a consultant takes the time to create an open space for a way out of the problem. The humanising effort of the consultant is to (help to) slow down and live through the problem. Like Socrates, described by Henri Bergson, a consultant is never satisfied with a final solution, because every solution is temporary and on its way to new problems, challenges and lines of flight. 'It seems to me that intuition often behaves in speculative matters like the demon of Socrates in practical life; it is at least in this form that it begins, in this form also that it continues to give the most clear-cut manifestations: it forbids. Faced with currently-accepted ideas, theses which seemed evident, affirmations which had up to that time passed as scientific, it whispers into the philosopher's ear the word: impossible!' (Bergson, 1968, p. 129). We no longer believe our words and trust the answers, but start asking questions, listen and enter into open dialogue beyond goals and targets.

It is a human search for temporary solutions, steering clear of mechanical outside-in solutions that help to discover what works. Not by recreating life in static answers and protocols born from an urge for efficiency, goals and targets, but by life itself, as the creative force in organisation. People and things are moving and are being moved. The humanising task of the consultant is to slow down, be tentative and sensible and to open up a space to search for solutions as lines of flight. This humanising effort of consultants helps to open up for the unexpected and the possible by having an eye for what is not yet there and staying clear of a final solution.

Notes

1 See Chapter 2 by Kaulingfreks in this book
2 Moreover, both the lean approach and Taylorism base their ideas on the context of car production lines. See also Taylor (1997); Ohno (1988); Chiarini (2012a; 2012b); Womack and Jones (2003); Liker (2007).
3 Gibson Burrell points at the absence of philosophy in standard Management Theory, which he indicates as *Heathrow Organisation Theory*: the management books available at most airport bookshops.
4 See, for instance, Fuglsang, M. and B.M. Sørensen (eds.) (2006); Sørensen, B.M. (2003, 2004, 2005); Pedersen, M. (2008); Kristensen, A.R., Pedersen, M. and Spoelstra, S. (2008).
5 Cf. De Landa (2006); Patton (2006).
6 Deleuze calls this the dynamics of deterritorialisation and reterritorialization that sets connections free in order to create new connections and thus creates new organisational processes (cf. Deleuze 2004).
7 To solve comes from the Latin word *Solvere*, which means to detach/to disconnect or to redeem/to save.
8 The work of Deleuze and Bergson have a preoccupation with "movement" and "time" in common. In his work Bergsonism (1991), Deleuze uses the work of Bergson as starting point or tools for developing his own concepts.
9 Styhre states that often knowledge is invoked as a fixed body of knowledge that can be employed for the benefit of the organisation: 'Knowledge is like a stock of knowledge at hand, ready to use (…)' In Bergson's view knowledge is never a stock, a fixed set of capabilities, skills or resources that can be used like any tangible resource. Knowledge is instead as a process, evolving and continually changing when put into practice' (Styhre, 2003, p. 23).
10 Both O'shea (2002) and Lazzarato (2007) argue that there is a difference between innovation and invention. The first being organic, living knowledge creation, the second being inert fabrication of

products. Quite often, the human capacity of knowledge creation is confused with the fabrication of products. For instance in the work of Nonaka and Takeuchi (1995).
11 For a deeper understanding of the cinematographical see Scott Ruse (2002); Olma (2007); Purser and Petranker (2005); Linstead (2002); Thanem and Linstead (2006); Calori (2002).
12 Cf. Gaffney, 2010, p. 87 and further, where he discusses the impact of Bergson's critical ideas about scientific knowledge and its relation to Deleuzian philosophy. In Bergsonism (1991) Deleuze connects Bergson's ideas about scientific knowledge to the concept of the virtual. Also see: Massumi, B. (2002) *Parables for the virtual: movement, affect, sensation*. Durham/London: Duke University Press.
13 www.kickstartyoursocialimpact.nl/
14 Parasense is related to 'paradox': para – beyond and doxa – opinon, or common sense. Spoelstra regards Parasense as a creative force in organisations (Spoelstra, 2007, p. 26).
15 In a Heideggerian sense related to aleitheia as a phenomenological or hermeneutical relational way to gather knowledge.
16 The problem as such can be regarded as a plenum, an empty space that is filled by multiple perspectives, interpretations and discussion. One could visualize a plenum as a square (*place* (French) or *plein* (Dutch)); the emptiness of the square makes it possible to fill it with perspectives, discussion and meaning.
17 *Lines of flight* is a Deleuzian concept that is used to indicate 'a way out', which can be fleeing as well as fleeing or leaking or disappearing into the distance (a vanishing point).

References

Bergson, H. (1968) *The creative mind*. New York: Greenwood Press.
Bergson, H. (1998) *Creative evolution*. Mineola, New York: Dover Publications.
Bergson, H. (2001) *Time and free will:, an essay on the immediate data of consciousness*. Mineola, New York: Dover Publications.
Bergson, H. (2004) *Matter and memory*. Mineola, New York: Dover Publications.
Burrell, G. (1989) 'The absent centre, the neglect of philosophy in Anglo-American Management Theory,' *Human Systems Management* 8 (4), p. 307–12.
Calori, R. (2002) 'Organisational development and the ontology of creative dialectical evolution,' *Organisation* 9 (1), p. 127–50.
Chia, R. (1996) *Organisational analysis as deconstructive practice*. New York/Boston: de Gruyter.
Chiarini, A. (2012a) *Lean organisation: From the tools of the Toyota Production System to Lean Office*. Milan: Springer.
Chiarini, A. (2012b) *From Total Quality Control to Lean Six Sigma: Evolution of the most important management systems for the excellence*. Milan: Springer.
Churchman, C.W. (1967) 'Wicked problems', *Management science* 14 (4), p. 141–142.
De Landa, M. (2006) *A new philosophy of society: Assemblage theory and social complexity*. London & New York: Continuum.
Deleuze, G. (1991) *Bergsonism*. New York: Zone Books.
Deleuze, G. (2004) *Difference and repetition*. London/New York: Continuum.
Deleuze, G. and Guattari, F. (2004a) *A thousand plateaus*. London/New York: Continuum.
Deleuze, G. and Guattari, F. (2004b) *Anti-Oedipus*. London: Continuum.
Fuglsang, M. and Sørensen, B.M. (2006) *Deleuze and the social*. Edinburgh: Edinburgh University Press.
Fuglsang, M. and Sørensen, B.M. (2006) Deleuze and the social: Is there a D-function? In: Fuglsang, M. and Sørensen, B.M. (eds.) (2006) *Deleuze and the social*. Edinburgh: Edinburgh University Press, p. 1–17.
Gaffney, P. (ed.) (2010) *The force of the virtual: Deleuze, science and philosophy*. Minneapolis/London: University of Minnesota Press.
Kristensen, A.R., Pedersen, M. and Spoelstra, S. (2008) 'Symptoms of organisation', *Ephemera: Theory and Politics in Organisation* 8 (1), p. 1–6.
Kunneman, H. (2005) *Voorbij het dikke-ik, bouwstenen voor een kritisch humanisme*. Amsterdam: Uitgeverij SWP.
Lazzarato, M. (2007) 'Machines to crystallize time: Bergson', *Theory Culture Society* 24 (6), p. 93–122.
Liker, J. (2007) *The Toyota way. 14 management principles from the world's greatest manufacturer (the company that invented Lean Production)*. New York: McGraw-Hill.

Linstead, S. (2002) 'Organisation as reply: Henri Bergson and casual organisation theory', *Organisation* 9 (1), p. 95–111.
Linstead, S. and Mullarkey, J. (2003) 'Time, creativity and culture: introducing Bergson', *Culture and Organisation* 9 (1), p. 3–13.
Massumi, B. (2002) *Parables for the virtual: movement, affect, sensation*. Durham / London: Duke University Press.
Nohria, N. and Beer, M. (2000) 'Cracking the Code of Change', *Harvard Business Review* May–June.
Nonaka, I. and Takeuchi H. (1995) *The knowledge creating company, How Japanese companies create the dynamics of innovation*. New York/Oxford: Oxford University Press.
O'Shea, A. (2002) 'The (r)evolution of new product innovation', *Organisation* 9 (1), p. 113–25.
Ohno, T. (1988) *Toyota Production System: beyond large-scale production*. London: Taylor and Francis Inc.
Olma, S. (2007) 'Physical Bergsonism and the worldliness of time', *Theory Culture Society* 24 (6), p. 123–37.
Patton, P. (2006) 'Order, exteriority and flat multiplicities in the social', in: Fuglsang, M., & Sørensen, B.M. (eds.) (2006) *Deleuze and the Social*. Edinburgh: Edinburgh University Press, p. 21–38.
Pedersen, M. (2008) 'Tune in, break down, and reboot–new machines for coping with the stress of commitment', *Culture and Organization* 14 (2), p. 171–85.
Purser, R.E. and Petranker, J. (2005) 'Unfreezing the future: exploring the dynamic of time in organisational change', *Journal of Behavioral Science* 41 (2), p. 182–203.
Rittel, H. and Webber, M. (1973) 'Dilemmas in a general theory of planning', *Policy Sciences* 4, p. 155–69.
Scott Ruse, M. (2002) 'The critique of intellect: Henri Bergson's prologiue to an organic epistemology', *Continental Philosophy Review* 35, p. 281–302.
Sørensen, B.M. (2003) 'Gilles Deleuze and the intensification of social theory', *Ephemera: Theory and Politics in Organisation* 3, p. 50–58.
Sørensen, B.M. (2004) *Making events work: Or, how to multiply your crisis*. Copenhagen: Samfundslitteratur.
Sørensen, B.M. (2005) 'Immaculate defecation: Gilles Deleuze and Félix Guattari in organisation theory', *The Sociological Review* 53 (1), p. 120–33.
Spoelstra, S. (2007) *What is organisation?* Lund: Lund Business Press
Styhre, A. (2003) 'Knowledge as a virtual asset: Bergson's notion of virtuality and organisational knowledge', *Culture and Organisation* 9 (1), p. 15–26.
Styhre, A. (2004). 'Rethinking knowledge: A Bergsonian critique of the notion of tacit knowledge', *British Journal of Management* 15, p. 177–88.
Taylor, F. (1911) *The principles of scientific management*. New York: Dover publications Inc.
Thanem, T. and Linstead, S. (2006) 'The trembling organisation: Order, change and the philosophy of the virtual', in: Fuglsang, M., and Sørensen, B.M. (2006) *Deleuze and the Social*. Edinburgh: Edinburgh University Press, p. 39–57.
Toppin, G. and F. Czerniawska (2005) *Consulting: a guide to how it works and how to make it work*. London: Profile Books Ltd.
Womack, J. and Jones, D. (2003) *Lean thinking: Banish waste and create wealth in your corporation*. New York: Simon & Schuster.

4 Humanisation, technology and organisation

Myrte van de Klundert and Robert van Boeschoten

Everyday technology

In present day society it is it is hard to find organisations, profit, non-profit and public alike, that do not in some way or another depend on or at least make use of information and communication technology (ICT). Since the end of the twentieth century there has been heated debate on ICT, with optimistic and pessimistic speculation on the future.[1] Today, however, the network society has become a reality: our social lives, organisations and economy heavily depend on ICT (Frissen and de Mul, 2008). ICT has become an everyday phenomenon, not only for most individuals in their private lives, but especially for organisations and the people working within them.

Despite the ordinariness of ICT there is still a concern for what we call the dehumanising effects of ICT in organisations. For example there is a critical discourse in education stating that human goals and relationships are made subordinate to technological systems, especially related to measurement (Biesta, 2010; Kohn, 2011; Jansen 2009). Coeckelbergh (2012) discusses how feelings of alienation may still occur, even though our daily lives are infused with technology.[2] Coeckelbergh describes alienation in this sense as encompassing a loss of engagement and feelings of meaninglessness. Another illustration is the popularity of the work of Richard Sennett on craftsmanship (2008) referring back to the Arts and Crafts workshops of the nineteenth century. Many are attracted to his ideals of good work where personal, small-scale involvement is leading. Across all sectors, increasingly, we find an alternative discourse on putting human values first (for example, Martin, 2011). We see this as a call for humanisation.

However, these discourses often place 'human values' in opposition to technology. The term humanisation is used in humanistic studies, and humanistic advisory work, to denote developments toward more humane organisations. Ideals of humanisation are often based in humanist anthropologies (images of man or human nature). For example, if the essential characteristic of the human is to use reason and to give meaning to everyday life and work through reasonable dialogue, then humanisation is the process of developing reasonable and dialogical organisations. Dehumanisation is then a form of alienation: to become removed from or unable to express this essential humanity that one has. Such a humanist outlook does not always cope well with the role of technologies. Technology is seen as instrumental, something external to the 'real' human processes of life and work (Verbeek, 2009). But technology, specifically ICT, is such a part of our daily lives, that any call for less or no technology seems nostalgic romanticism.

At the other end of the spectrum, there is a transhumanist ideal of humanisation. These are the futuristic ideals of transcending the current human for something entirely new or at least something 3.0 (see for example Kurzweil, 1999, or the popular work of Silva, 2015). Basically, technology is still instrumental, not part of the human. Technology is what will help us transcend our human deficiencies, or the human as we know it will be overcome altogether, computed into technological singularity (Kurzweil, 1999; Vinge, 1993). Humanisation is the process of becoming better humans. This seems both unrealistic and a bridge too far to many because here, the deficient human stands in opposition to technology, and the human comes off the worst and is subsumed.

In this chapter we make a journey with French philosopher Bernard Stiegler. We take a middle road, steering clear of both extremes, leading to a theory of humanisation that takes concerns as raised above seriously *and* does not subsume technology to the human and vice versa.

First we will discuss a philosophical anthropology that relates the human and the technical/technological, following Stiegler. We will discern technics (as skill) from technology (the discourse on technics, techno-logics). We will discuss briefly how ethics and autonomy can be seen from this perspective. Then we propose how this theory is a theory of humanisation, and assess how this compares to the essentialist and transhumanist ideals mentioned above. Because the proof of the pudding is in the eating, we discuss the example of ICT in educational organisations.

Technics as skill: the anthropological question

In the twentieth century philosophers have started to pay more attention to technology. Characteristic of the first currents in this field is that technology is discussed monolithically, as if all technics can be understood as having the same essence. These views are largely pessimistic: technology alienates us from authentic ways of life. These philosophies were very human-centred. These three aspects have been under attack. Newer theories look at the effects of specific artefacts. Often, these theories state that humans and things are fundamentally related. Some go very far, stating there is no difference between humans and things, or, that humans are cyborgs.

In such a view, Coeckelbergh (2012) argues, there is no possible problem of alienation. After all, if we are related at the ontic level, that is to say, at the level of what we and things *are*, how could we be alienated from the world or ourselves by technology? In the next section, we expand on what this means for a theory of humanisation and dehumanisation and its relation to humanist ideas of humanisation and alienation.

What would a more acceptable perspective on the relationship between the human and the technical look like? In this section we will outline Bernard Stiegler's basic scheme as laid out mainly in his magnum opus *Technics and Time* (1994, 1996, 2001). Stiegler prefers not to call himself a philosopher of technology (Lemmens, 2011). He has written about capitalism, globalisation, cinema, education and many other topics. For our purposes here, five concepts suffice to tell the story of the human: technics as skill and the difference between technics and technology, individuation, organology, autonomy and pharmacology.

Stiegler writes, 'The human and the tool invent each other. There is something like a technical maieutics' (Stiegler, 1998, p. 175). How is that possible? It makes sense to say the technical does not exist without the human,[3] but it is not self-evident that the human does not exist without technology. As tool-inventing beings, by accident more than by intention, people develop skills. Such skills make variable ways of life possible. Just try to think of a human way of life without skills that involve material tools: for cooking, washing, etc. Such skills are not given or natural. People have to *learn* everything that they do throughout their lives: to eat, to speak, to handle a spoon, to read, to write, or to type, to like, to click, to check in, etc. A skill is a technique, a capability to apply technics. Technology is the logic/logos of the skill. Technology relates the effects of techniques to a certain purpose. For example, someone taught me the skill of using a hammer. The technology of this skill is to forge a relationship between two elements, let's say wood and nail, through the activity of hammering. The logos of a technique becomes its technology as a form of discourse, 'a discourse on technics' (Stiegler, 1998, p. 93). So technology, other than technics 'per se', makes clear what a skill is all about; it shows its consequence for the way we understand the world as something we can engage with in this way or that. It is through this technology that we are able to understand our world differently and create new ideals for our society.

What the learning of skill brings with it is imagination and desire. There is no given, natural way to live. By experiencing different ways to engage with a world – by making a world – human beings develop desire to become or to have something (again) through the use of technics. Humans thus always have the potential for becoming something new, something other, and are constituted by their relationship to this other-to-come to which they relate through technology. Stiegler explains this in reference to the myth of Prometheus (1998). Prometheus' brother, Epimetheus, gave all living beings special gifts. He forgot to give the human a specific quality with which to sustain itself. Prometheus then gave humans technics. With technics, the human has to sustain itself, make something out of itself.

This process of becoming is called individuation. It is a process of realisation of potentialities, without ever exhausting those potentialities. It is based in imagination: projection of a future on the basis of one's experience. That is, on the basis of some interpretation of one's past, but also simply the experience that remains in the body. When you have learned how to use a hammer and nail, it becomes possible to make realistic projections about something you want to make. On the basis of experience we project possibilities for ourselves and work on reaching our goals, ideals, etc. Because we are skilled at something, we are capable of such projection. This ideal of our selves is not individualistic. The relationship between the skill to create something and the technology by which we engage with others to envision a future world are connected. Imagination is grounded in the dialogue on technology and the skill of each person.

This leads to a certain image of the human. One might say, humans are lacking. They have a deficiency; they do not 'naturally' know how to live. One could look at this in a different way. Humans have a certain degree of freedom. They are capable of the new, of exceeding their biological programmatic. They can experience a difference between the past and the present: they can experience having become something other than before. The skill is grounded in how it deals with a certain material. Applying skill leaves traces in the material which makes us aware of the past. The experience of difference is a condition for projecting oneself into the future. Humans can imagine their own becoming, which is not programmatically set out by nature. Humans are not just what they are by nature; they are always becoming, developing their potential, which is inexhaustible because technological development is inexhaustible. So the nature of the human cannot be explained without referring to what is external to humans. The dialogical core that humanists so often see as an essence is to be placed in the *relationship* between the human and its material surroundings, its tools, *and* the social realm in which those tools are developed and through which people relate.

Placing skill and learning at the heart of the human means placing technology and the social at the heart of the human. Thus it is technology that makes humans historical: the stories about why certain techniques were more important than others and how these techniques enabled a society to develop in a certain way.

To understand individuation, it is crucial to understand that within Stiegler's framework, the individual does not exist without the social and the technical. Because skill has an external component, the learning achievements of the individual are accessible to others, who further develop the technology and skills.[4] The individual is always dependent on others for growing up and becoming autonomous. For a social group to persist over time *as* a singular or distinct group – let's say a culture or an organisation – it is necessary that there is some shared skill, some technologies through which people may recognise each other.

So, a group of people that somehow belong together also individuate. They are in the same kind of process of becoming based in their technological milieu. What most people call culture, Stiegler refers to as transindividuation (see especially Stiegler, 2012). Just think of everything that is specific about a culture: it is always related to specific tools with which shared meaning is created. Humans are historical beings, because of the possibility of handing down skills that have some material basis. We can still remember Greek society and what they knew because of the skills and technologies that conserve traces of this past - reading, writing, artefacts – through which we can imagine this as our past. Humans are social beings, because we can do nothing without having learned some basic skills form others at some point. Humans are cultural beings, because of the possibility of handing down knowledge, stories, and identities, through the techniques we share. How could a culture or organisation (or organisational culture) exist without a material basis in which its heritage is developed over time, without individuals continually (trans)forming their future on the basis of this past? Transindividuation and individual individuation co-constitute on each other.

Autonomy and ethics

The relationship between skill, technology, the individual and the social has some interesting consequences. Ethics is one of the points where individual and social meet in skilled activity. When I am skilled, it is possible to act ethically. Without any idea of the effects of my actions, how can I judge what is right, whether I am harming someone, etc.? Ethical judgement itself becomes a skill based in time and experience. What is right is itself based on the norms developed over time which are interiorised through the learning of skills and through the way technologies have become part of the society.

One way to frame this, as Stiegler does, is through the lens of autonomy. To Stiegler (see especially Stiegler, 2013), autonomy depends on imagination that is created through time, which is constituted through the skilled use of technology. Every new technique makes us heteronomous; we are subjected to its demands. To give a simple example: learning to write, a child needs to learn to restrain movements. A child is not all at once able to use a pen and to write a story. But over time, more experience makes one skilled at the use of this technique. This basis then makes it possible to imagine what one could do with it. It becomes possible to *desire* something, and to work to achieve something. This is what autonomy means: being capable of desiring something projected on the basis of some experience and working to achieve it. This is why Stiegler connects autonomy to care (for oneself and each other, see Stiegler, 2010). So the first stage in dealing with new technologies is adaptation (subjection); the second stage is adoption (care).[5] Adoption means how to *care* for that with which we are confronted, both the techniques and ourselves as we are becoming in relation to them.

Autonomy and heteronomy are not opposed though (Stiegler, 2013).[6] Autonomy is not achieved once and for all after learning something. First of all, every new capacity brings some form of incapacity. But also, autonomy and heteronomy are two sides of the same coin (the process of individuation). This principle Stiegler calls, in accord with French tradition, pharmacology. Every technique is a therapeutic poison. Anything that may be a medicine with which we care for ourselves and each other may become a poison. Since humans are bound to use technologies as skill, humans are pharmacological beings. Because of technics we may care for each other and ourselves, but it is a form of care that is always at risk of failing. It gives us potential, which we are always at risk of not realising.

In summary, humans are not just *beings* who are what they are by some given internal constitution with which they are born. They are *open*. They always have the potential to become something else, to learn new skills; they are becomings. This is possible because humans depend on techniques, in relation to which they learn skill. As Coeckelbergh puts it, technology is skilled purposeful activity (p. 210). No skill exists without a technological artefact, something material. Technologies make time possible. The discourse on the effects of techniques that create all kinds of projects in a society also create a history of imagination. Because we can experience development we experience ourselves in time, and thus we can imagine a future and desire more than what our instincts dictate (as far as we could know what our instincts are at all). Ethics, involving judgement on relationships and consequences of action, is based in skill; it requires a form of autonomy, of choice, that is only realised in relation to technology.

Humanism, humanisation and technology: translation

Now it's time to translate the theory just described into a theory of humanisation. To make this move we will rely on Peter Derkx' description of humanism, which is fairly representative for present-day Dutch humanism.

To describe humanism, Derkx relies on the first notations of the term humanitas and humanus by Renaissance thinkers (2011, p. 18). They used the idea of humanity both descriptively and normatively at the same time. The core of humanism consists of four essential features, according to him: (1) all worldviews are contextual and of human making (and thus one cannot rely on God to solve human conflict), (2) all human beings have dignity (descriptively) and should respect and express this dignity (normatively), (3) human beings can (descriptive) and should (normative) develop themselves, and (4) we should love and care for unique, irreplaceable individuals (no human may be made subordinate to some abstraction). Humanisation is only defined once, hastily, as working on the expectations, needs, desires and ideals in relationship to social and natural surroundings (p. 76).

Humanisation is a humanist ideal: the active side of humanism, always implying both a description of the human, and taking this human to be normative. Humanisation means some humanity can and needs to be developed. The charter for human rights is based on this normative ideal. People like Martha Nussbaum have used this to explore and describe the grounds for this normative action (2011). We are always already human, and yet this humanity is always a potential that needs to be developed, working at our expectations, needs, desires and ideals in relationship to our social and natural surroundings. Since our contexts change, the process of humanisation is never ending.

Stiegler does not speak of dignity, or any other central value, as a categorical *essence* of the human. However, in many other respects Stiegler's theory fits in well with this humanist idea of humanisation. His discussion of the process of being human is both descriptive and normative. The principle of (self)development is as central to his thinking as the notion of individuation (although he does not reserve the term individuation for only the human, similar to Simondon (1989)). However, he not only describes individuation as normative but also contends that certain conditions can be formulated for this process to happen. That is what he calls the organology: there are organological conditions to individuation, meaning the individual, social and technical all individuate and depend on each other for their development. The idea of dignity and respect for each other's dignity – equality – may be read into this idea. The opposite of individuation is individualisation: the elements are cut loose from each other and can no longer contribute to each other's development. No new potential is raised and thus cannot be developed. The potentiality of the human is thus not given as fundamental, inherent dignity.

What it means to be human is a potential raised in the process of development of the elements in a threefold 'organological' relation. In Derkx' words this would mean that if people disappear within the system, they become completely subordinated to abstractions of social imagination or technical systems and dehumanisation takes place. Or in Stiegler's terms, the organology breaks down and the therapeutic skilled activities that make up a culture become poisonous or obsolete.

In summary, humanisation is a never-ending process that is always individual, social and technical at the same time. The difference between humanist ideals and Stiegler's perspective is that the latter does not give a positive, essential potential to aim for. There is no essence to strive for just a process of being, and yet this gives us things that Western thinking has tended to recognise as typically human: freedom, dialogue, care, etc.

Technics, and in its wake technology, is thus very central to humanisation, contrary to humanist views. Changes in technics/technology change the potential to become something we desire to be. Also, autonomy, which is important to our story of ICT and organisations, is thus socially (as recognised by humanists) and technically (as generally not recognised by humanists) supported. We need skills, adopted technics, to be autonomous, to be able to imagine the consequences of our actions, desire one consequence above the other, and act accordingly. Such technics are by definitions always social, because they are developed over time and have social histories. Thus, the other way around it is also true: in caring for oneself and one's desires through skilled activity, a care for society could be implied.

Applying the humanisation perspective to education: management and ICT

Why is the reputation of management in education so much under fire lately and what does this have to do with the introduction of so many ICT projects?[7] The revolt by students and educators alike at Dutch universities in the beginning of 2015 are all directed towards a 'calculating' management. People recognise possible value in ICT, but are angry about dehumanising tendencies: the quality of their work is being reduced to financial profitability and the organisation of their work is moving from a concern for pupils to administrative tasks (Ilomäki, 2008). The value they create with their work is reappropriated by management through obscuring systems of control. How this is made possible has a lot to do with the way ICT is being applied by management.

Stiegler speaks of a technology as a logic created by certain techniques. If we look at the logic of ICT we see that it standardises and individualises.[8] The technique of computer coding makes all particulars distinct from all others. The techniques consist of bits and bytes as distinct unities that are part of the programming language, which produces typical results with regard to specific goals. It cannot be interpreted like ordinary language, where the meaning of words arises out of a certain context. The program defines beforehand what needs to be addressed, and leaves out other possibilities. Meaning appears as something that fits the program. This produces a logic based on recognition and creates an image of transparency and efficiency. For managers these qualities are very attractive. It gives a sense of control over what needs to be done and it makes clear how the organisation needs to reach its targets.

This so-called transparency offered by ICT is also criticised as part of the policy of meritocracy (Tonkens and Swierstra, 2008). Everyone needs a fair chance to reach his or her potential and transparency is needed to show how these chances can be created. Individualising the scores one needs to achieve in order to be recognised by the organisation mainly creates transparency here. To know what a good score is the organisation needs to standardise output. The Organisation for Economic Cooperation and Development (OECD) has done this for a comparison in education between nations: the Program for International Student Assessment (PISA) score (OECD.org). Nations are treated as separate particulars that can be compared because they all have the same goal: good education. But good education seen through the eyes of the OECD looks very different from what nation states and educational institutes within these nations aim for. If we look at the demands of educational employees in the highly symbolic location of the Maagdenhuis in Amsterdam (spring 2015), one of the core elements is that people wish to be judged by standards *they* recognise to represent value.

ICT helps organisations such as the OECD to promote their cause by showing results from the PISA scores as windows of opportunity for education to strive for. But economic outputs related to how efficient an organisation is operating are not the only forms of imagination in education. Educators usually have concern for their pupils and formulate different goals like *Bildung*. In order to achieve this they use different skills like dialogue and co-construction of projects, much like the workplace of the craftsman. The imagination of becoming a professional in a certain field requires training that makes use of strong involvement between pupils and educators. To make clear what a person can be in our society and strive for certain positions within this society, specific goals become very different from one another. To bring this all together by one score does not do justice to the complexity of these demands. For their work ICT can be relevant as well as part of community building or feedback construction to strengthen the relationships between pupils, or between themselves and the pupils. This kind of imagination related to ICT is usually not part of the discussion in the management room. Educators need to be involved with their pupils and need to be able to see a pupil as an individual with his/her own process of development that the educator needs to stimulate. The result of this process cannot be preprogramed but is part of the interaction between educator and pupil. It is an open process. Educators thus feel left out and isolated by management who only give credit for preprogramed targets. Their techniques used in teaching have become irrelevant; their results are measured according to standards – measured by techniques – they do not recognise and have not adopted. Thus in Stiegler's terms they are individualised instead of individuating.

Taking care of ICT in education

The challenge for managers in education is to see how different forms of imagination related to ICT can be brought into a dialogue that would enable the organisation to include all stakeholders. Making the technique of creating particulars that are used for measurements the dominant quality of ICT frustrates the organology that is central to developing a culture of care in education. An organology can only blossom when the processes of interaction between individuals and interaction within the group are related to the techniques that are used. Management should be aware of the consequences of techniques for stimulating a culture of involvement. Not only the individuals in the organisation but the organisation itself can only grow into its next phase of development when the imagination related to the techniques used by all individuals within the organisation is discussed in an open dialogue.

Another characteristic of ICT is that it speeds up processes of change within the organisation.[9] Software programs are regularly updated because they need to be more encompassing and more efficient. The desire/imagination, as written above, is stimulated by ever more transparency and efficiency, bringing the whole organisation into the realm of clear and specific targets as part of management goals. In the beginning ICT in education was mainly used to measure results of pupils but very soon it had to measure other forms of output as well. Educators are asked to import figures into programs (standardisation) that automatically create stats that indicate average output (individualisation). Every year new software is introduced which demands adjustment and takes time to become familiar with. Educators do not get the time to get to know the programme and adopt it so it can be made part of their ambitions and imagination. This leads to having to work with systems to which you are subordinate. Educators become, as Flusser stated, mere operators (Flusser, 2011). In this way, following Stiegler's paradigm, ICT makes educators heteronomous. Some even go so far as to identify their position as that of coolies (Jansen, 2009), showing the darker side of being an educator in contemporary society. Educators seem to be stuck in between as subalterns, on the one hand doing what is demanded of them by the organisation in an administrative way, but on the other hand in need of recognition of what they are trying to achieve with their pupils/students, which is not part of the administration, as outlined in the argument before. Again, this stimulates a process of individualisation where meaning becomes hard to find instead of individuation. The challenge to develop oneself into an autonomous being, relating to a professional field of expertise, *takes time*. These tools require new skills that you have to learn. Unfortunately time to learn is often not given by management in education due to the pressure of becoming more efficient and cost effective.

The skill of educators is important for them as an ethical ground for taking care of future generations. Being skilled means being able to judge the consequences of your actions, at least to a minimal degree. Having to work with new tools thus creates a situation in which an educator is not capable of producing 'good work' (Ewijk and Kunneman, 2013) in an ethical sense, even if the result fits the goals the tools were used for. If you cannot foresee the effects you produce, it has become impossible to act ethically. Skills and imagination go hand in hand. Organisations need this imagination of professionals grounded in skills to develop humanisation processes. It needs to organise a ground for dialogue among different groups in the organisation to make clear how skilled work is being produced. The different ideals related to these skills enable the formation of a future scenario for the organisation to live by.

Some concluding remarks

Humanisation within the standard literature on humanism is usually framed in one of two ways in relation to technology. In both positions the human is opposed to the technical.

In this chapter we showed that the human could be seen as grounded in technology, making humanisation also a technical process. Common central notions of humanisation like dialogue still have a central value, but in this case based upon a hermeneutical relation between individuals, society and technology. Imagination based on skill creates opportunities for the organisation.

Stiegler gives us preconditions for humanisation that differ from what has been used before where the human is the only ground for developing human values. Autonomy, imagination and ethics have become part of a different framework for humanisation. Organology is central to Stiegler's concept of transindividuation that produces *human values*. The individual, the collective and technology coproduce this organology as an ongoing process of development creating continuously new values. Organisations are challenged in bringing these three elements in a constant dialogue to produce imagination for future projects.

In the example we analysed, we concluded that by applying Stiegler's concepts new perspectives and actions are possible. An essential problem in education is that the imagination of management produced by ICT has been put at the forefront for the organisation as a whole. A collective imagination is forced upon all the other professionals, thereby appropriating the values created through the skills of the educators. Efficiency and transparency are made central to all in the organisation, which blocks the individuation process of others and therefore also the transindividuation (culture) of the organisation. In opposition to others who share the same concern, such as Biesta (2010), Kohn (2011) and Tonkens and Swierstra (2008), it is not a dominant ideal grounded in skills that leads to the use of certain technologies but certain technologies that inform our ideals.[10] Making this shift in perspective leads to other ideas about managing organisations. A collective imagination is still needed but instead of being uniform this should be versatile, acknowledging diversity and being more open to what can be accomplished.

Looking at the organisation from a humanising point of view means in Stiegler's terms that there should be a concern for time needed to appropriate skills. Technology develops continuously and offers many possibilities for an organisation to apply, but value is only created when the people that have to work with it adopt this technology. As Stiegler indicates, it takes time to go from adjusting to adopting.

Notes

1 Wellman and Haythornthwaite (2002, p. 2–4) show how in the early days of the Internet, this new technology spawned wild euphoric speculation on how this was to change the world. See also Berners-Lee and Fischetti (1999). Recent critical authors point out the increasing control and loss of privacy, such as Lanier (2013), Morozov (2013), Turkle (2011).
2 See for example Coombs, Knights and Willmott, 1992; Ragu-Nathan et al., 2008.
3 According to Colony (2011), this is a very anthropocentric tendency in Stiegler, against which good arguments could be made concerning the gradual difference between humans and animals.
4 The technical term here is epiphylogenesis. Stiegler's ideas about the biological basis of intergenerational learning and the interiorisation of techniques are in part based on Wolf (2008). See also Carr (2011).
5 In *Science and Technology Studies* this process is often referred to as domestication, for example as described by Van den Akker and Kool (2012) as following a pattern of commodification, appropriation and finally conversion.
6 Of course multiple philosophical perspectives have been developed on technology. Peter-Paul Verbeek (2014a, 2014b) argues that we are always entwined with technologies (hybridity) because they change our situation and thus make it impossible to formulate our ethics autonomously as if we were not already related to it.

7 Within academia there has been a growing debate on how to assess achievements in research and teaching especially within the humanities departments. Many university boards (Amsterdam, Missouri, Montreal, Sydney) have faced protests from students and staff alike opposing the cuts in courses and in favor of diversity in training.
8 Individualisation by technology is a topic that has been often studied. Wellman and Haythornthwaite (2002) maintain that new communications technology (especially the Internet) has led to networked individualism. People are not based in communities or places, but reachable as individuals through the technologies that connect them to others. As Stiegler notes, people are always connected through technics/technologies, but the individualising character of many ICT systems used in organisations do not allow for this to lead to community. As Jose van Dijck says, communication media are best understood as connectivity, and yet they are 'weapons of mass distraction': they do not lead to working on ideals, developing desires, etc. (see van Djick [2015] youtube.com). Different aspects of individualisation as used in social studies, such as structural versus cultural (based on Inglehart, 1977 and Putnam, 2000), are summarised well by van de Veen, Yerkes and Achterberg (2002, p. 196).
9 In search of the causes of a perceived decline in civic disengagement, Robert Putnam notes the extraordinary speed with which new appliances are developed and adopted by households (2000, p. 217). He is famous for describing the trend of individualisation that comes from certain new technologies that simply invite us to use them on our own (chapter 13). He discusses this for television especially, stating that it leads to a decline in civic engagement, both through the effect of the medium and through its specific content (p. 242–243).
10 In Dutch literature on ICT, the account of de Mul (2002) is very informative. Regarding the informatisation of our worldview, they argue for an interactionist account where ICT and the people using it change/influence each other.

References

Berners-Lee, T. and Fischetti, M. (1999) *Weaving the web: The original design and ultimate destiny of the World Wide Web by its inventor*. Britain: Orion Business.
Biesta, G.J.J. (2010) *Good education in an age of measurement: ethics, politics, democracy*. Boulder: Paradigm Publishers.
Carr, N. (2011) *Het ondiepe. Hoe onze hersenen omgaan met internet*. Dorset: Maverick Publishing.
Coeckelbergh, M. (2012) 'Technology as skill and activity: Revisiting the problem of alienation', *Techné* 16 (3), p. 208–30.
Colony, T. (2011) 'Epimetheus bound: Stiegler on Derrida, life, and the technological condition', *Research in Phenomenology* 41, p. 72–89.
Coombs, R., Knights, D. and Willmott, H.C. (1992) 'Culture, control and competition: Towards a conceptual framework for the study of information technology in organizations', *Organization Studies* 13 (1), p. 51–72.
Mul, J. (ed.) (2002) *Filosofie in cyberspace: reflecties op de informatie- en communicatietechnologie*. Kampen: Klement.
Derkx, P.H.J.M. (2011) *Humanisme zinvol leven en nooit meer ouder worden. Een levensbeschouwelijke visie op ingrijpende biomedisch-technologische levensverlenging*. Brussels: VUB press.
Flusser, V. (2011) *Into the universe of technical images*. (Trans. N. A. Roth). Minneapolis: University of Minnesota Press.
Frissen, V. and de Mul, J. (eds.) (2008) *De draagbare lichtheid van het bestaan. Het alledaagse gezicht van de informatiesamenleving*. Kampen: Uitgeverij Klement.
Ilomäki, L. (2008) *The effects of ICT on school teachers' and students' perspectives*. Turku: Painosalama Oy.
Inglehart R. (1977) *Modernization and postmodernization: Cultural, economic, and political change in 43 societies*. New Jersey: Princeton University Press.
Jansen H. (2009) *De leraar als Koelie, postmoderne kritische pedagogiek*. Amersfoort: Agiel.
Kohn, A. (2011) *Feel-bad education: And other contrarian essays on children & schooling*. Boston: Beacon Press.
Kurzweil, R. (1999) *The age of spiritual machines: When computers exceed human intelligence*. New York: Viking/Penguin Group.
Lanier, J. (2013) *Who owns the future?* New York: Simon and Schuster.
Lemmens, P. (2011) '"This system does not produce pleasure anymore": An interview with Bernard Stiegler', *Krisis Journal for Contemporary Philosophy* 1, p. 33–41.
Martin, G. (2011) *Human values and ethics in the workplace*. Sherrybrook: G.P. Martin Publishing.

Morozov, E. (2013) *To save everything, click here: technology, solutionism, and the urge to fix problems that don't exist*. London: Allen Lane/Penguin Group.
Nussbaum, M. (2011) *Creating capabilities: the human development approach*. Cambridge, Massachusetts: The Belknap Press of Harvard University Press.
Programme for International Student Assesment (PISA). *Organisation for Economic Co-operation and Development* (OECD) (online). Retrieved 7-3-2015. www.oecd.org/pisa/
Putnam, R. (2000) *Bowling alone: The collapse and revival of American community*. New York: Simon & Schuster.
Ragu-Nathan, T.S., Tarafdar, M., Ragu-Nathan, B.S. and Tu, Q. (2008) 'The consequences of technostress for end users in organizations: Conceptual development and empirical validation', *Information Systems Research* 19 (4), p. 417–433.
Sennet, R. (2008) *The craftsman*. New Haven: Yale University Press.
Silva, J. (2015) *Singularity Hub* (online). Retrieved 2-3-1015. http://singularityhub.com/tag/Jason-silva/.
Simondon, H. (1989) *Du mode d'existence des objets techniques* (second edn.). Paris: Aubier.
Stiegler, B. (2010) *Taking care of youth and the generations* (Trans. S. Barker). Stanford: Stanford University Press.
- (2012) *Disbelief and discredit. volume 2: uncontrollable societies of disaffected individual* (Trans. D. Ross). Cambridge: Polity.
- (2013) *What makes life worth living: On pharmacology* (Trans. D. Ross). Cambridge: Polity.
- (1994) *La Technique et le temps: La faute d'Épiméthée*. Paris: Editions Galilee.
- (1996) *La Technique et le temps: La désorientation*. Paris: Editions Galilee
- (2001). *La Technique et le temps: Le temps du cinéma et la question du mal-être*. Paris: Editions Galilee
- (1998) *Technics and time 1: The fault of Epimetheus* (Trans. R. Beardsworth and G. Collins). Stanford: Stanford University Press.
Tonkens, E. and Swierstra, T. (eds.) (2008) *De beste de baas? Verdienste, respect en solidariteit in een meritocratie*. Amsterdam: Amsterdam University Press.
Turkle, S. (2011) *Alone together: why we expect more from technology and less from each other*. Boston: MIT Press.
van den Akker, R. & Kool, L. (2012) 'Buiten de gebaande paden of binnen het eigen straatje? Geosociale netwerken en de orkestratie van toeval', in: Van't Hof, C. and Timmer, J. (eds.) (2012) *Voorgeprogrammeerd. Hoe internet ons leven leidt*. Den Haag: Boom Lemma Uitgevers.
van de Veen, R., Yerkes, M. and Achterberg, P. (2002) *The transformation of solidarity, changing risks and the future of the welfare state*. Amsterdam: AUP.
van Djick, J. (2015). 'Social media and the culture of connectivity', *Center for 21st Century Studies* (online). Retrieved 7-3-2015. www.youtube.com/watch?v=x-mdi63Zk58.
van Ewijk, H. and Kunneman, H. (2013) *Praktijken van normatieve professionalisering*. Amsterdam: SWP.
Verbeek, P. -P. (2009) *Cultivating humanity: Towards a non-humanist ethics of technology*. New Hampshire: Palgrave MacMillan.
- (2014a) *Op de vleugels van Icarus. Hoe techniek en moraal met elkaar meebewegen*. Rotterdam: Lemniscaat.
- (2014b) *The moral status of technical artifacts*. Dordrecht: Springer.
Vinge, V. (1993) 'The coming technological singularity: how to survive in the post-human era', *Whole Earth Review* 77, p. 11–23.
Wellman, B. and Haythornthwaite, C. (eds) (2002) *The Internet in everyday life*. Oxford: Blackwell Publishing.
Wolf, M. (2008) *Proust and the squid: The story and science of the reading brain*. London: Icon Books.

5 The humanisation of education
Teaching the wisdom of uncertainty

Martien Schreurs

Introduction

Learning is always accompanied by uncertainty. For both students and supervisors this uncertainty is hard to endure. In our meritocratic society a control paradigm is dominant. In order to reduce uncertainty, students are directed by well-described procedures and checklists. Although this brings assurance that they are on the right track, it diminishes the creative learning potential that emerges from uncertainty. In this chapter I argue that uncertainty is not a problem to be solved, but a key to Bildung. Within educational science, the concept of Bildung is defined as 'a creative process, in which a person, through his or her own actions, shapes and "develops" himself or herself and his or her cultural development' (Siljander and Sutinen, 2012, p. 3). When students go through the process of Bildung, there are no guarantees. Rather than providing assurance, the learning process aims to result in the wisdom of uncertainty. This wisdom builds on the continuous emergence of new, more fruitful perspectives. In order to facilitate Bildung, the educational process should confront students with a diversity of perspectives and paradigms. A turn towards Bildung in education has huge implications for management in educational contexts. Managers should create more balance between active control strategies and mindful acceptance of the unavoidable uncertainties that accompany learning. I label this creation of more balance as the humanisation of education.

Education and uncertainty

All caregivers, whether they are parents, health care providers or teachers, have a responsibility to ensure the development of the child's basic trust. Children that can rely on their parents or caregivers and on predictable daily routines develop a sense of safety (Erikson, 1968). Their needs are met and there are fixed times for playing, eating and sleeping. In the daily ritual of a bedtime story, children are (re)assured that they live in a just and righteous world. After all, in the end, the 'bad guys' in the stories are always punished and 'the good' live happily ever after. Children that grow up in an emotionally safe place are privileged with a basic trust. This trust is a foundation on which they can build during their life course. This is what Giddens (1991) calls *ontological security*. Without this underlying ontological security, children are less able to take risks and to explore new possibilities. In other words, they are less able to cope with the uncertainties in life.

Sooner or later, all people are confronted with events that don't fit their presumptions and that shatter their notions of a predictable world. Giddens (1991) calls these crucial events 'fateful moments'. During these fateful moments basic trust is confronted with existential uncertainty. Whereas children need to be reassured, adolescents and adults need to learn to cope with the uncertainties of life. How can people learn to cope with this existential uncertainty? In this rapidly changing world, this is a question that the field of education must address.

However, education seems more prone to impose order and structure on students and to teach evidence-based knowledge than to cultivate tolerance for uncertainty. In the past, the high status of the professors was enough to enable students to develop a basic trust in the world. The common belief was the professor knows best. Nowadays this kind of trust is no longer *embodied* in professors and professionals, but *organised* in standards and protocols. Standardised measures are instrumental means to provide security. Underlying these standardised measures is the belief that learning processes are both predictable and controllable. Therefore education could and should be well structured in line with learning objectives. Examination should be insightful and transparent. Test results should be categorised by strict and distinct standards. For the sake of the quality of education, students are asked to evaluate every course by filling in a standardised form in which they themselves give grades to the different parts of the course, including the teaching qualities of their professors. In this highly administrative and managerial discourse, quality is quantified. Transparency is the norm: both professors and students are publically held accountable for their performances.

This chapter aims to demonstrate that students are more and more socialised and disciplined into a technocratic discourse that strives for control, standardisation and certainty. In a sense, this contemporary technocracy serves the same purpose as the religions of the past, namely the striving for order and certainty. This striving for order and certainty suppresses the enigmatic aspects of life that can never be organised, measured and controlled. However, uncertainty can never be totally exiled. Beneath the surface there are always existential and moral issues that remain unresolved. Not only are there fundamental questions about the meaning of life, at a more practical level lots of uncertainties and insecurities also remain. Students are confronted with a lack of guarantees, for instance in the labour market where there are not enough jobs available for all of them. Moreover, in their working environments the 'specifics' make it impossible to fully work according to protocols and standards. People have to be able to (re)act responsibly in a world that is fundamentally uncertain. Individuals have to make choices and this comes with a burden of responsibility.

Experiences of existential and practical uncertainty and insecurity are often hidden behind a veil of objectivity. And yet, these issues will remain. When we don't address our existential questions, we're subject to 'Seinsvergessenheit' (Heidegger, 1927): we forget what life, in its essence, is all about. Humanisation of education presupposes the acknowledgement of the existential uncertainties and critical reflection on how to cope with these challenges. These reflections are not only the students' or the professors' concern, but are also highly relevant for leaders and managers in the field of education.

The main challenge in humanising educational organisations is to balance control with the acceptance of uncertainty. This chapter demonstrates the practical implications of the one-dimensional emphasis on control to both students and professors in an academic context. A reflection on a specific example aims to clarify that the emphasis on control is fed by dominant accountability structures in the field of education, in which both professionals and managers are subjected to output measures. This chapter argues that both professionals and managers need to rehabilitate 'the wisdom of uncertainty' (Kundera, 1988) as a benchmark for humanisation of the field of education.

Setting the debate: an example

Wherever highly educated professionals meet, there is usually someone who criticises procedures. In a particular situation a supervisor at the Dutch University for Humanistic Studies expressed his concerns about side effects of the instrumentalisation of the processes of writing and supervising bachelor theses. Students who write their bachelor theses are subjected to strict procedures and in-between assessments of (parts of) their theses. The supervisors are expected to use standardised criteria on a number of checklists. This particular supervisor explained his worries that students who are constantly monitored and given feedback would not feel responsible for their own efforts. According to him the external guidance by checklists and standards undermined intrinsic motivation because, in practice, such guidance provokes an outsourcing of their responsibilities. In order to ignite further reflection on the topic, he stressed his opinion in an e-mail correspondence with his colleagues:

Dear colleagues,

(…) So, we control the process by giving formative feedback and eventually summative feedback. Our coaching is intense and disciplined. But meanwhile I observe the side effects of this disciplining. Our students become more and more dependent on our feedback. Their work is half-baked and they wait for our guidance. They are afraid to think for themselves. Here's my objection: while the supervisors are working harder and harder, students become more and more passive until the point that they become task performing monkeys. I want to stress that this passiveness of students is unintentionally conditioned by our external guidance. Contemporary universities show similarity to secondary education. Even though this control discourse is dominant in The Netherlands, we, as a University for Humanistic Studies, should reflect on the question whether it is congruent with our humanistic view on learning. Humanists stimulate students' intrinsic motivation, curiosity and autonomy. We are at risk of getting estranged from our own ideals.

Yours sincerely

One of his superiors responded:

Dear colleagues,

Unfortunately I couldn't attend yesterday's meeting, but I have a different opinion regarding the intensive feedback on the students' work. I don't consider this as control or disciplining, but as teaching craftmanship. I am always impressed by the way doctors (and possibly lawyers and judges) learn their profession: by getting lots of daily feedback, short evaluative moments: what went well and what needs improvement? That's the way to learn craftmanship. Of course we don't want half-baked products from our students. We need to be strict and hold them accountable for the quality of their work (if it is really bad, we should deny their papers). But even when they perform well, they can always do better.

Yours sincerely,

…

Apparently the superior in this example strongly believes in the functionality of the use of checklists and systematic feedback at fixed intervals. However, if the process of guiding a student to write a bachelor thesis is fueled by preset categories and is reduced to ticking the checklists, then there is no fundamental reflection about the goodness of fit between the criteria and the purpose of the thesis. This reflection should be part of the dialogue between student and supervisor, whereby the latter attunes to the unique learning process of the student. The supervision should 'open up' rather than 'close down'. Such an open learning process accepts uncertainty instead of reducing it. It is through the acceptance of uncertainty that the potential for creativity abides.

So, seen in this light, uncertainty is not a problem that needs to be resolved by the supervisor. Managers should not expect supervisors to take away the students' uncertainties by explicating their expectations, because this comes at a high cost of a loss of students' competencies to cope with fundamental uncertainty and a loss of creativity. Unintentionally, we teach our students not to long for creativity and adventure, but to strive for structure. We turn education into a kind of industrial production rather than providing ground for innovative craftsmanship (Sennet, 2008). Not only managers, but also students are in need of clear expectations and of reduction of uncertainty. This is illustrated by the following e-mail from a student ambassador to the teacher of a course.

Dear Sir,

In response to some complaints of my fellow students regarding the sequence of the presentations and the papers that we're supposed to hand in for your course, I, as student ambassador, would like to address this topic. A couple of students wondered why the presentations were planned before the final deadline of the papers. It seems more reasonable to hand in the paper first, because then you're guaranteed of the professors' approval of the content of the presentation. Spending all of your time on a presentation without being sure if you're on the right track seems like a waste of time to some of us. What is the rationale behind this sequence? I suppose you've made an intentional decision and I would like to communicate this with my fellow students.

Sincerely yours,

…

This e-mail informs us of the students' need for certainty provided by external control. They seem dependent on the teachers' approval. Apparently, it is hard for them to endure the insecurity that accompanies their performance. They are so obsessed with external incentives and formal criteria that they no longer feel responsible for their own aspirations, let alone that they dare to rely on their own judgments. It seems as if students have 'outsourced' their responsibility. They seem to believe that their work is successful once it has met external demands. In the field of educational studies this is referred to as 'the hidden curriculum'. Educational scientists define this hidden curriculum as 'the unstated norms, values and beliefs that are transmitted to students through the underlying structure and meaning (…) in the social relations of the school and classroom life' (Langhout and Michell, 2008, p. 595). For instance, although a professor can claim that he wants the students to form their own opinions, in practice the students might learn that an opinion that is in line with the professor's opinion gets more approval (Giroux and Penna, 1979; Langhout and Mitchell, 2008).

Moreover, an unintentional side effect of clinging to checklists and standardised procedures is that they form an obstruction for informal dialogue between supervisors and students. Rather than engaging in dialogue with their supervisors, the students check the assessment forms. Thus, the ideal of Bildung is overruled by an instrumental approach and the students become calculative. The calculative student tries to reach for the best results with the least uncertainties. In case things go wrong, the system is to be blamed rather than the work itself. In addition, the students are required to work efficiently within predefined time slots. Thus, through standardising, monitoring and incentivising the writing of a thesis, students are more or less conditioned to behave like *homo economicus*.

Education in a meritocratic society

Homo economicus is the 'enfant terrible' of our meritocratic society with its characteristic performance management (New Public Management). A meritocracy is a society in which the power is held by the people who have earned their positions by their accomplishments. Within the field of educational science a meritocracy is defined as 'a social system where individual talent and effort, rather than ascriptive traits, determine individuals' placements in a social hierarchy' (Alon and Tienda, 2007, p. 489). It is in this light that we can gain a deeper understanding of the emphasis on control in education. Education's primary task is to empower individual students, to enable them to participate in a meritocratic society, where they are responsible for making their own choices. A meritocratic society thrives by comparison: one's social position is based on merits. Testing, competition and control are essential elements in a meritocracy and, thus, it is not surprising that they are also strongly embedded in the field of education. In our meritocratic society there is a strong need for an objective and systematic approach towards learning processes: 'the existence of meritocratic ideals presumes there is a consensus on what merit is, and that the multidimensional construct of merit can be adequately, if not accurately measured' (Alon and Tienda, 2007, p. 489).

While in the past the final professional judgment of a professor was enigmatic and beyond discussion, nowadays so-called 'transparency' is the norm. With an argument that looks to prevent subjectivity and arbitrariness, procedures and assessment criteria are standardised and professors are held accountable for their assessments.

The rise of New Public Management has led to an educational straightjacket of performance measures. Professors are held accountable for their performance by external standards that are forced upon them by top-down policies. The government is the primary investor into education and demands its money's worth. Therefore, the contracts between the government and universities are set in terms of performance measures. Professionals and managers, with their hands and feet tied, are bound to these external guidelines. This has a strong impact on the organisations' vision on professionals' responsibility. Responsible behaviour has become more or less synonymous with accountable behaviour. But there is a fundamental difference between responsible behaviour in a community and being accountable against external performance standards that are imposed on professionals in an organisation. These performance standards are the central topics of appraisals. When targets are not met, both manager and professional are expected to 'take responsibility' in the sense that they will do their best to meet the targets in the future. For instance, they are expected to meet publication targets or to get better evaluations by students. This form of instrumental accountability creates calculable or governable individuals. A calculable individual is made to act by extrinsic motivators. It is the expectation of a reward (in whatever sense) or the threat of a punishment that mobilises calculable men. As research (Frey, 1997) shows that an overload of extrinsic motivators may decrease the level of intrinsic motivation, this has a negative impact on the commitment of people towards their profession or their organisation. It moreover downplays morality. Morality is 'swallowed' by the drive to produce results and to meet targets. Individuals become anxious or opportunistic through an emphasis on 'Self' rather than on the profession or the organisation. They become economic men rather than committed men. We have reached the point where accountability towards external performance standards has supremacy over our professional commitment with the Bildung of students. This 'economization of education' is a societal transformation that is described by Biesta (2010) as the transformation from welfarism towards new managerialism. Biesta makes a distinction between three levels of transformation, namely (1) the transformation of students into costumers, (2) the transformation of democratic consultation into a technical bureaucratic culture of blaming and (3) the transformation of professional knowledge into an evidence-based approach.

In this transformation, all teaching activities without pre-specified outcomes have become a priori suspect. Uncertainty is hard to bear in a technocratic time-area and culture in which exact sciences, technological professions, law schools and business economic studies thrive so much more than the humanities. The humanities, after all, have an inherent orientation towards values and ideas that are beyond the realm of objective knowledge (Nussbaum, 2010).

Acknowledging uncertainty

A shift from control towards the acceptance of uncertainty requires a turn away from objectives and standard setting towards values and norms. It requires the recognition that learning objectives are embedded in overarching and abstract values such as citizenship or Bildung. Although in Western society there is a deep consensus regarding the urgency of Bildung and citizenship in education, it is often problematic to translate these hypergoods[1] into explicit learning objectives. Because of this, objectives are often formulated as measurable competencies. In this context, the Dutch historian Bregman and the Dutch economist Frederik (2015) characterise the educational discourse: 'It's always about skills, never about values. It's always about didactics, never about ideals. It's always about problem solving, never about the problem itself.'[2] We seem to have lost the fundamental insight that the question as to what it means to teach and learn with qualitative depth is really a question without final and objective answers. Managers try to reduce the uncertainties regarding this question by transforming education into something that is controllable and auditable. This performance management is implemented throughout all layers so that it permeates everything. For example, policies aim at discouraging students to opt for a major that has few job guarantees, and financial incentives are used to limit the time span of studying. Because they have no study time to lose, it comes as no surprise that students long for certainty, discipline and structure. This policy is legitimised by the idea that students have few intrinsic learning aspirations. It is a common thought that additional time would only be wasted on partying. But learning and especially Bildung take time, the kind of time that cannot always be accounted for, the kind of time that doesn't produce measurable results, the kind of time, in other words, with uncertain outcomes. These uncertain and often hard to measure outcomes are undervalued. Management is obsessed with reaching preconceived targets, but if everything is under control, it leaves no space for unexpected wisdom to emerge from uncertain trajectories.

Our meritocratic society and technocratic culture are characterised by a deep existential desire for security. Since the advance of science, technology and economics, there is a widespread neglect of existential uncertainties. Many have come to believe that we can only know what we can measure. This is why the positivistic mainstream scientists like to quote Wittgenstein (1921): 'Whereof one cannot speak, thereof one must be silent'.[3] The Czech writer Milan Kundera acknowledges that it's hard for people to endure the essential relativity of human things. There are no clear guidelines for dealing with moral and existential uncertainty and so it is tempting to ban these questions from the domain of science. This is the case in mainstream psychology with its exclusive focus on visible human behavior and measurable human traits. Another example is economics, which has, since the 19th century, turned from a moral and political science into a quantitative science. Again, the insecurity of moral considerations is 'swallowed' by the perceived security of quantitative calculations. Hard figures and colorful spreadsheets are more convincing than the uncertainty of moral reflection that is evoked by narratives and deliberations. The 'objectivity' that we project onto hard figures and spreadsheets appeals to our desire for certainty. But behind a veil of illusionary certainties and facts there is a dimension of sense making. This domain is characterised by uncertainty: there always remains a possibility of another perspective on human matters. This defies our need for control and clarity. Because of this, Kundera says, the wisdom of the novel, which is essentially the wisdom of uncertainty, is difficult to accept and understand (Kundera, 1988).

Right here, professional teachers have a huge responsibility. In order to restore Bildung, educational professionals must acknowledge uncertainty. To humanise education means to acknowledge and to do justice to the unruly human condition. What is needed is a fundamental reflection on the values of education and a revisiting of the aims of specific educational programs. How can professors teach the students to cope with contingency and uncertainty? How can managers create spaces for Bildung?

Bildung: teaching the wisdom of uncertainty

In order to restore the value of 'responsibility' rather than 'accountability', to emphasise authenticity rather than calculability, future education has to accept a big challenge. Levinas defines responsibility as the willingness to respond to the appeal of the other. True responsibility implies moral questioning and the outcome of such questioning is necessarily uncertain.

Responsibility is intertwined with dialogue. From the time of Socrates, dialogue means mediated voice (Dia = through, logos = word). When we apply a dialogical framework to pedagogical undertakings, we can do justice to the human condition that is in essence ambiguous and uncertain and for which no teacher can provide 'The Answers'. According to pedagogue Jones (2014), the teacher appeals to the responsibility of the student to undertake this uncertain dialogical process together. Jones (2014, p. 487) stresses that there will always be risks and uncertainties in the dialogical relations between students and teachers, because a genuine dialogue can neither be planned nor controlled. It arises within a relation, denoting that it is constituted in the line of encounter between the student and the subject and is therefore unpredictable. Dialogue doesn't only involve intelligence but foremost intellectual capacity. This distinction between intelligence and intellect is well described by the historian Hofstadter (1963). He defines intelligence as an excellence of mind that can be applied, in relatively narrow ways, to practical problems. Intellect is more philosophical and is characterised by contemplation, criticism, creativity, and attention to further consequences, to being at home among complexities and the bigger framework of the bigger picture. The intellectual sphere is a domain of questioning that is inevitably accompanied by uncertainty. This is in line with Biesta's view on wisdom. According to him wisdom is particularly important in order to capture that our educational actions are never just a repetition of what has happened in the past but are always radically open toward the future. 'We need judgment rather than recipes in order to be able to engage with this openness and do so in an educational way' (Biesta, 2014, p. 137). What students need to acquire is 'the wisdom of uncertainty' (Kundera, 1988): trusting that their intellectual quest will contribute to the emergence of new, more fruitful perspectives.

By learning to cope with uncertainty, students learn to change their points of view. They broaden their horizon and creativity can emerge (Biesta, 2014). When students value uncertainty and see it as an opportunity to gain new insights and understandings, they recognise its learning potential. For educational purposes, this implies that students have to be confronted with diversity. Diversity necessarily evokes uncertainty, whereby students come to realise that there is no 'point of Archimedes' that reconciles all differences in opinions or perspectives. The point is to teach students to relate to the uncertainty that comes with this huge diversity of perspectives. The role of the teacher is vital. To stimulate an intellectual dialogue, he must be curious and cultivate an openness of mind. The encounter between a teacher and his students can always be in some sense a new beginning (Levinson, 1997, p. 450). Systems of accountability tend to stand in the way of such new beginnings. The results of pedagogical efforts focused on new beginnings are always uncertain. This 'pathos of the new' is what Hannah Arendt calls natality: an open adventure that we must embrace.

In order to teach the wisdom of uncertainty, we can turn to the long humanistic tradition of Bildung. According to Schellhammer (2014, p. 5), '(…) Bildung is a dialogical term'. It is inextricably linked to plurality and dialogue: 'Bildung entails the open and curious confrontation with this multifaceted world.' This learning potential is actualised when a confrontation with uncertainty leads to the exploration of new perspectives. The ideal of Bildung calls teachers to guide this uncertain process, instead of reassuring the students that there is only order and structure.

Conclusion and recommendations

In learning to cope with uncertainty, there are no guarantees for success. In this sense this plea for the wisdom of uncertainty contradicts the managerialism described above. In the field of education there is a misbalance between the striving for control and the endurance of uncertainty. It makes no sense, however, to ban the culture of accounting and control altogether, because its efficiency cannot be denied. A problem arises when control strategies deny the domain of uncertainty. This domain of uncertainty withdraws from control strategies. It is beyond the sphere of direct influence. Uncertainty brings with it a potential for learning and creativity. Thus, humanisation of education entails the acknowledgement of the unavoidable uncertainties in life. We need to create more balance between active control strategies and mindful acceptance of uncertainties. This striving for balance is exactly the pursuit of the humanisation of education.

Therefore, the main recommendation to the managers in the field of education is that they allow students and professors time and space for Bildung. This implies the (re)valuation of uncertainty. I define Bildung as learning to cope with uncertainty. The first step that must be taken is that school managers take a self-critical look at the existential fears that are at the base of their control strategies. The intolerance for uncertainty seems to be fueled by mistrust. When managers are afraid to place their trust in professors' intrinsic motivations, they impose all kinds of control strategies on them. In the section 'Setting the debate' we observed that this results in the implementation of standardised checklists leaves little room for professional autonomy.

If this atmosphere of distrust slowly gives way to trust, then professors and students alike can work to find their inner strengths or intrinsic motivators – creativity and responsibility – which can then function as an inner compass. If the professors manage to teach students to cope with uncertainty, then the accompanying sense of accomplishment will be richer than anything we can achieve with the aim of control and certainty.

Notes

1 Charles Taylor (1992) defines 'hypergoods' as the fundamental, architectonic goods that serve as the basis of our moral frameworks.
2 Bregman & Frederik, 2015, p. 51: 'Het gaat altijd over vaardigheden, nooit over waarden. Het gaat altijd over didactiek, nooit over idealen. Het gaat altijd over "probleemoplossend vermogen", nooit over wat die problemen dan precies zijn.'
3 wo von man nicht sprechen kann, darüber muss man schweigen.

References

Alon, S. and Tienda, M. (2007) 'Diversity, opportunity, and the shifting meritocracy in higher education', *American Sociological Review* 72, p. 196–223.
Biesta, G. J. J. (2010) *Good education in an age of measurement: Ethics, politics, and democracy*. Boulder, CO: Paradigm Publishers.
Biesta. G. J. J. (2014) *The beautiful risk of education*. Boulder, CO: Paradigm Publishers.
Bregman, R. and Frederik, J. (2015) Waarom vuinismannen meer verdienen dan miljonairs. In: Bregman, R. and Frederik, J. (eds.) *Waarom vulinismannen meer verdienen dan miljonairs*. Amsterdam: Stichting maand van de filosofie, p. 37–53.
Erikson, E. (1968) *Identity: Youth and crisis*. London: Faber.
Frey, B. S. (1997) 'A constitution for knaves crowds out civic virtues', *The Economic Journal* 107, p. 1043–53.
Giddens, A. (1991) *Modernity and self-identity: self and society in the late modern age*. Stanford, CA: Stanford University Press.
Giroux, H. A. and Penna, A. N. (1979) 'Social education in the classroom: the Dynamics of the hidden curriculum'. *Theory and Research in Social Education* 7 (1), p. 21–41.
Heidegger, M. (1927) *Sein und Zeit*. Tübingen: Max Niemeier Verlag.
Hofstadter, R. (1963) *Anti-intellectualism in American life*. New York: Knopf.
Jones, L. (2014). 'Learning as calling and responding', *Studies in Philosophy and Education* 33, p. 481–493.
Kundera, M. (1988) *The art of the novel*. New York: Grove Press.
Langhout, R. and Mitchell, C. (2008) 'Engaging contexts: drawing the link between student and teacher experiences of the hidden curriculum', *Journal of Community and Applied Social Psychology* 18, p. 593–614.
Levinson, N. (1997) 'Teaching in the midst of belatedness: the paradox of natality in Hannah Arendt's educational thought', *Educational Theory* 47 (4), p. 435–51.
Nussbaum, M. (2010) *Not for profit: why democracy needs the humanities*. Princeton, NJ: Princeton University Press.
Schellhammer, B. (2014) *Dialogical self as prerequisite in concepts of intercultural adult education*. Paper concerning the content of a Workshop during the Eighth International Conference on the Dialogical Self, The Hague, The Netherlands.
Sennet, R. (2008) *The craftsman*. New York: Yale University Press.
Siljander, P., & Sutinen, A. (2012). Introduction. In Siljander, P., Kivelä, A., & Sutinen, A. (Eds). *Theories of Bildung and growth* (p. 1–18). Rotterdam/Boston/Tapei: Sense publishers.
Taylor, C. (1992) *The sources of the self*. Cambridge: Cambridge University Press.
Wittgenstein, L. (1921) *Tractatus logico-philosophicus*. New York: Harcourt, Brace and Company.

6 Leadership and humanisation in a forensic psychiatric clinic

Gabriël Anthonio and Myrte van de Klundert[1]

Introduction

According to Aristotle, true virtue always holds the middle ground between two vices. An administrator in a vertically arranged organisation, who treats her employees as cogs in a machine leaving no room for human self-direction, is unsound. At the other end of the spectrum we might imagine completely horizontal organisations where laissez-faire leadership does not provide any vision at all, which is also unsound. Freedom and discipline presuppose each other (Huijer, 2013). What is the middle ground in organisations, the right balance between clear boundaries of vertical administration and sufficient self-direction in the horizontal space? How to judge this tension?

This will obviously depend on the specific circumstances of an organisation and its clients. Humanisation offers a helpful perspective.

In this chapter I discuss the problems and questions involved in the humanisation of a forensic psychiatric clinic, where I was CEO for eight years. What once started as the humanisation of prison systems threatens to turn into the opposite. New rationalised forms of control, discipline and protection once were definitely a humanising trend, but today rationalisation and bureaucratisation are leading to new forms of humiliation – of clients as much as of employees. What is the right balance between freedom and discipline? How does a manager find this balance?

From a humanist perspective I see humans as twofold beings: capable of self-direction but always relationally embedded. Humanisation is the practical philosophy of humanism. Humanism takes this image of the human to be both descriptive and normative. Relational autonomy is constitutive of human dignity. Human lives are fragile – autonomy and relations are constantly under pressure and threat of dehumanisation. But because people are autonomous, humanisation can only be a process of ongoing development of autonomy and relationships; it can never become a system into which people can be forced.

A historical sketch: humanisation of the prison system

The first mentions of humanisation in the Dutch language concern criminal law and specifically the prison system. Two trends are important. During prior centuries reflection on power relations increased; self-direction and dignity became foregrounded leading to better treatment. Reflection on power relations gradually increased; self-direction and dignity became foregrounded leading to better treatment. Accordingly, more and more damaging practices were left behind; humiliation, torture and solitary incarceration decreased.

For centuries, transgression would lead to total exclusion, torture or death. With cultural perceptions of the human changing in the fifteenth and sixteenth century, perspectives on punishment changed too. After discipline in the form of expulsion, corporeal punishment, public humiliation and torture decreased, while cellular confinement increased. In the humanist revival during the Renaissance there was prison reform. Dirk Volkertszoon Coornhert (1522–90) was one of the first reformers to openly question what sensible punishment could be both in terms of execution and of meaning. His book '*Boeventucht*' (punishment of criminals) was based on humanist principles like dignity, and it was based on his personal experiences during exile and detention (Bonger and Hoogervorst, 1989). As an ally of William of Orange who led the revolt against Philip the Second, he was forced to flee, and for a short period was detained in the prison of The Hague. Based on this experience Coornhert critically argued against unnecessarily added inhumane punishment of solitary incarceration, social exclusion, discipline by guards, a ban on speech, restricted daylight and airtime and a diet of water and bread.

Coornhert's influential writing led to the foundation of the first grating houses. In these houses detainees would grate red, tropical wood to be used for the colouring industry (Lissenberg, van Swaaningen and van Ruller, 2001). Instead of detention people could labour under surveillance. After the grating houses in larger cities, other workplaces were installed for different industries, like weaving and agriculture. In the first instance mostly women and adolescents were given access to these alternative punishment systems. Workplaces for adult men were developed later. As time went by, attention to the well-being of prisoners increased, with pastoral care, medical care and even, starting on a very small scale, education. So the self-reflection of power led to humanising reforms.

After the Renaissance detainees were no longer seen as objects of punishment and discipline. More and more, criminals were taken to be (partially) the product of their environment, in need of education instead of punishment. As this contextual/sociological view became more dominant, even the already more humane cellular incarceration was pressured. The climate of punishment and education within the prison system functioned as a mirror for changing cultural perceptions.

After the terror of the Second World War the humanisation process was given a new impulse. People within the legal and medical professions who had been incarcerated in concentration camps fought especially diligently for humane and dignified detention on humanist or Christian grounds. Criminologist and rehabilitation officer Kempe, who had been detained as a political prisoner, argued in 1946 against solitary confinement and the ban on speech. Kempe called the airing spaces, where prisoners would walk in line without speaking at all, and the solitary cells, 'rabbit cages'. Again, an influential position, intellectual capacity and personal experience were crucial in the process of humanisation. In what followed this humanisation process, attention grew for re-socialisation and education. Besides humane treatment, efforts were made to prepare inmates for their reintegration.

A relational perspective thus was established over time and an expression of this assumption of relatedness in the prison system was fought for by means of bureaucratic legislation. Regulation in this case protected the individual and restrained power.

The public social order

Is this humanisation process unique to the context of prison systems? Organisations are structurally engaged with humanisation. Every organisation restrains self-direction and yet gives opportunities for self-development, working on ideals and being with others. Scharmer and Kaufer (2013) propose all organisations could, and should, move from ego- to eco-directed organisations that foreground people and their well-being, instead of profits and shareholder value. They state classical management positions and the concomitant hierarchical structures for rational decision making should make room for an awareness of humanity, sense making and spiritual values. Along many sectors, public and commercial, many organisations are experimenting with concepts and forms that are supposed to substitute inhumane, vertical power structures for less alienating ways of working together based on dialogue and human well-being (Kolind and Botter, 2014). There is now a steady flow of literature on examples of successful self-direction in organisations that cut down on bureaucracy and control (Jansen et al., 2009).

For organisation within the *public* social order, such as in education, hospitals or boarding houses, humanisation poses even more urgent problems and questions. On this terrain there is also an increasing awareness of the theme. Arguably, Martha Nussbaum's *Cultivating Humanity* (1997) can be read as a call for humanising higher education. She calls for more reflection and dialogue instead of a focus on purely professional knowledge, and for art, philosophy, literature and other liberal arts to get much more attention within all curricula.

Public organisations have an element of formal inequality. Their clients are not restrained in their self-direction by choice. It is in the nature of public organisations that people are not involved with them as clients voluntarily. They cannot leave to take their needs elsewhere. Their freedom is by definition pressured. And yet these organisations often see the empowerment of their clients as one of their goals. Their mission and responsibility is to leave as much space as possible for the self-direction of clients. This is what restrains their power. So public organisations constantly negotiate the tension between the vertical, hierarchical organisation and the responsibility to do justice to the capacity of people to lead their own life in a way that is meaningful to them. Thus, evaluating public organisations always involves assessing some operationalised form of self-direction in light of the organisational context (Ossewaarde, 2006, p. 43–4). The balance will be different for staff and clients in a hospital, school, prison or local government.

One of the trends of humanisation, as I mentioned, is the increase in self-reflection of power. Power is rationalised and its wielding restrained by more and more rules. The damage and humiliation of formal inequality is thus limited as much as possible. The power individuals have over each other becomes less absolute and their interactions come to be led by rational principles. This is humanising not just for 'clients' (students, the sick, inmates) at the lower end of the hierarchy. Generally it is perceived to be humanising for an organisation in its entirety as equality increases. Through bureaucracy the protection of the (rights of) clients and the power restrictions of employees/executives is embedded in organisational systems.

This however can bring new forms of dehumanisation in its wake. With the execution of power in modern public organisations we are no longer confronted with the indignity of being delivered into the hands of individuals who can treat us as they please. Power and discipline have become less visible, woven into standardised systems and bureaucratic regulations.

New dehumanisation

Working in an institution with a public nature generally means a lot more than just work and making a living for employees. People are often proud of their profession, and autonomous professional action often entails self-direction, personal development and making connections. Recognition and being valued by clients and society at large matter a lot in such professions. It is part of what makes work more than *just work* for teachers, administrators, nurses, social workers and the like. This kind of work often is part of what gives meaning to their lives. Such professionals these days often experience alienation and disempowerment, as is debated heavily in popular and academic literature. People experience demotivation, as well as physical and psychic health issues. As Dutch philosopher Verbrugge stated in widely recognised language: 'All too many teachers, doctors and nurses feel robbed of their profession. In the organisational models made up by their managers they have become anonymous externally controlled processors. This must change' (NRC, 18-06-2005, my translation).

This bureaucratisation (rationalisation) and verticalisation of organisations leads employees to imagine their hospital, school or prison as a Taylorist production system where they simply put together the parts. They feel that in such a rational organisation, they have become anonymous, unreflective, repetitive machines fulfilling their standardised, partial activities. Bureaucratisation and control mechanisms that foster such standardisation are proliferating. In professional action there is no room left for self-direction: instead of professional considerations, predictability, efficiency and profit dictate the course of action. The voices of the few brave employees who raise questions about the ethical content of such action are smothered in the dominant discourse of efficiency and productivity. The picture painted here reminds me of Charlie Chaplin's film of the production worker hardly capable of keeping up (*Modern Times*, 1936).

It is not surprising that a new discourse can be witnessed that resembles the old human relations theory. A flood of books and articles is rising about the theme of alienation from labour and organisations. In his book about 'Theory U' Otto Scharmer contends that organisations need a human face again, where people are the starting point and not systems or technologies (Scharmer, 2013). Wouter Hart argues in *Verdraaide Organisaties* (*Twisted Organisations*) (2013) that public organisations should return to their essential goals because rational organisations and their systems have become goals in and of themselves. Peters and Pouw (2004), on a more rhetorical note, compare rationalised public organisations to bio-industrial production of standardised outcomes without any meaning in either the process or the final result. Another example is *Beroepstrots* (*Professional Pride*) by Jansen, van den Brink and Kole, where, next to alienation of employees, specific attention is given to customers or citizens who use the services or products provided by public institutions (2009).

Rationalisation thus has both employees or professionals and customers or clients disappear, together with a public or common good. While managers develop more and more rules and systems, employees spend their time every day with many activities that do not make sense to them and defy their ideals. There is no space for self-direction, case-specific adjustments or innovation, and clients also miss this self-direction and the potential for actual relationships because this is based on actions that do not fit the assembly line. Those still feeling apprehension at such a situation should be considered lucky not to be numbed yet, but many have given up and go through their daily routines without ever reflecting. Human action is missing; people really do play the role of robots. Any problem arising will be incorporated directly by systemic intervention without any educative reflection or dialogue. In a vertical organisation people are not really part of the solution, because solutions are found in refining the rules and regulations. Rationalisation – starting out as humanisation – is reversed into its opposite.

In the following I will describe this tension between the horizontal and the vertical, freedom and discipline, self-direction and control, as it was apparent in the penitentiary institution during my time as CEO, and discuss how I negotiated it.

Case study: Dr. S. van Mesdag clinic

In 1997 I was appointed division manager of the Dr. S. van Mesdag clinic by the Ministry of Justice and from 1999 until 2005 I was the CEO. The clinic is a forensic psychiatric hospital. Inmates here have often undergone prison sentences before arriving and undergo compulsory treatment here, sometimes for an unknown length of time. The clinic was in big trouble. There was an eight million euro shortage, the buildings were in desperate need of renovation and labour absenteeism was at a staggering fourteen per cent. During 1997 two inmates had escaped, there had been four suicides in a row, and employees were accused of integrity failures, such as smuggling drugs and sexual transgressions (Ludwig and Blom, 2001). The Inspection for Health reported treatments were far below standards and the criminal investigation department stated the clinic had become an unsafe environment with heightened risk of transgressive behaviour of both staff and inmates. The board, advised by external consultants and the Department of Justice, had implemented interventions of a highly rational nature. Surveillance was reinforced, cameras were placed, the buildings were enhanced by North Atlantic Treaty Organisation (NATO) wire, parole and visits were controlled more strictly and solitary confinement was more often and more easily applied. Employees opposing the new regime were warned and told to adhere strictly to the new rules without question. This rational, controlling reflex was to calm the storm (Anthonio, 2006). Despite these measures the client board and employee board withdrew their confidence in the board. Negative media attention did not wane. Members of Congress publicly questioned the responsible ministers about the safety of the clinic. The crisis was all-encompassing.

The first reactions during the crisis, geared towards reinforcement of discipline and surveillance, did not counter the crisis. The verticalisation of the organisation encountered a lot of resistance from the media, clients and employees; there was a lot of talk of a culture of fear and control and the organisation was increasingly experienced as inhumane. The psychiatric clinic, which basically is a prison where people are treated for mental and behavioural problems, was invented as an extension of the humanisation trend. According to modern standards certain people need to be incarcerated, but treated for their illnesses. However, in such institutions, as Foucault already showed decades ago, new kinds of control mechanisms exert a very profound form of power, not just over bodies but over minds (Foucault, 2001). Especially in a psychiatric clinic, vertical, power-infused mechanisms can take over the whole organisation.

Humanisation as an opportunity?

I reported about the crisis and the way it was handled in my doctorate thesis *The Humanisation of a Justitial Organisation: Human Values as Guiding Principle for Organisational Change* (Anthonio, 2006). How did we go about managing the crisis? How did we achieve a much needed change in a positive direction?

First of all, we created a period and a space for reflection. My colleagues on the new board and I envisioned what direction the change should take: towards a more horizontal, human centred and humane organisation. 'The starting point of a humanisation process is and remains the human. The main strategy we followed was to have change not be implemented top down, or bottom up, but to have it grow from the inside, horizontally, taking form as we engaged in dialogue' (Anthonio, 2006, p. 11). This ideal crystallized into a positioning statement. Its central theme was to go from a culture of control towards a human-centred organisation with a culture of professional treatment. People from all levels of staff were involved in wording this ideal. It is inherently contradictory for a manager to feed an ideal of a 'human-centred organisation' into an organisation without engaging everyone in it – however inspired management is with her ideal! The ideal, sketched in the positioning statement, was placed on the horizon as a focus point (Anthonio, 2006, p. 154). I cite a few lines from this first statement:

> In our imaginary public organisation employees come to the clinic every day taking pleasure in their work. [...] All employees are satisfied with their salary, their role and their position within the organisation. [...] The climate is experienced as safe, challenging and stimulating. Anyone has opportunities to explore their talents, also when these are not mentioned in their job descriptions. [...]
>
> Management is involved, know their staff and are accessible. [...] The organisation is run by management who presuppose maximum self-direction of individual staff and teams. Decisions are made collectively. [...] The means (how to reach goals) are largely the responsibility of staff, the end (goals, results) are largely the responsibility of management. [...]
>
> The organisation has labour absenteeism of 2,5%, high productivity and profit. Clients judge us as excellent. [...] To the general public the organisation is known as innovative and trendsetting. The organisation constantly invests in improvement of products and services. [...] The principles of a healthy building harbouring a safe climate and open sphere are leading. As a learning organisation the clinic constantly improves. Jobseekers are really waiting in line to get a chance to work with us.

Positively stated, this ideal, human-centred organisation offers maximum space for self-organisation and innovation and it provides work satisfaction. Concepts like respect for patients and room for their own responsibility are guiding. The treatment should of course be professional and offer safety. In treatment the quality of contact and dialogue are central. From a security point of view power and oversight are central but our ideal organisation emphasises treatment rather that imprisonment.

Negatively stated the ideal is to not have a vertical, rational organisation where profit and production are central and people are treated as robots. The humane organisation is not only human centred but leaves behind inhumane treatment. Of course a completely 'human-centred organisation' as an ideal is exactly that: an ideal. But we can imagine it and let it be a central principle while managing the quality of products and services. Ideals cannot be realised but they may lead.

Against the backdrop of the crisis and this ideal picture, as board and staff, supported by the staff and client councils, we started looking for inspiration from helpful and regulative ideas and theories. The bones of the ideal we had constructed needed concepts to give it some flesh. Without this the concept would remain rhetorical. We found guidance from a number of theories we started to call 'sources'. Anyone could make suggestions and bring a theory into the conversation. We mapped out a route on the way to our ideal of this new, human-centred organisation with language and concepts that we could share.

Source: Goffman, structure and ethics

For a critical reordering of the processes, organisation and communication we found inspiration with Goffman (1977, 1993), who describes life in social institutions as theatre. A theatre has coulisses, a space for the director and actors. The stage is for the actors, supported by decorum and clothing. It is crucial for the actors and director to know each other's text, roles and positions. This upholds the façade, the magic, the illusion of the piece intended to be played out. The public does not need and does not want to know what takes place in the coulisse. An important demand of the public, besides the quality of the actors (managers) and decorum (the building, atmosphere), is congruence. As a whole, the piece should make sense, the parts relating to each other forming a complete show. In my thesis I devoted a complete chapter to the prison as a theatre with all its roles, positions and texts (Anthonio, 2006, p. 93–144). We were constantly tested: do we still make a convincing show, do the roles and text coincide with the announced route to a more human-centred organisation? Besides role and text, the building as decorum was changed. Art projects with the inmates were initiated, a new, friendlier colour for the walls was chosen, and the removal of unnecessary gates, bars and the infamous NATO wire were celebrated as important statements. Goffman's theory was not just used as a model for structuring our reality, it became a moral reference: were we doing what we said we would do, and were we doing it in unity?

Source: Margalit and respect

An inmate (in Dutch: *Ter Beschikking gestelde*, placed at the disposal of government) is a special category, but of course, first of all, a human being. To fill in this core thought of the humanisation process we delved into multiple sources. Above it was shown in the historical sketch that an institution of justice might teach us something about the level of civilisation in a given society. How one deals with punishment is, according to Avishai Margalit (1998, p. 229), still widely recognised as a test for dignity. To get humane values into view then, one might also look at what would constitute the inhumane. Goffman had already stated in his work on total public institutions such as prisons how these are capable of systematic humiliation. When people are systematically humiliated, by intimidation and neglect, this is seen as inhumane. Such a situation is characterised as inhuman or unworthy of human dignity. Margalit argues that a decent society resists those things that give reason for citizens to feel humiliated (Margalit, 1996, p. 20) He distinguishes two opposed, extreme positions that we take as signposts defining the way to a decent society (Margalit, 1996, p. 20–31).

The first position could be summarised from an anarchist perspective. It states that any restriction of autonomy or self-direction of an individual is humiliating: *regulative institutions are a legitimate reason for people to feel humiliated*. The second position flows from a stoic perspective. Here one would hold that external factors do not need to have any real impact on the well-being of individuals. In this case the ability of free thought overrules any aspect of possible physical restraint: *regulative institutions are no reason for people to feel humiliated at all*.

Margalit is convinced that our search for a decent society steers between these extremities (Margalit, 1996, p. 34). We translated this into a concept of the humane organisation. After all, what goes for a society might hold for an organisation. Institutions with a regulative character, like the prison system, education and health care are part of this society and need to negotiate the same tension between horizontal and vertical dimensions. Accordingly, the middle ground was summarised as follows: *regulative institutions, such as the Dr. S. van Mesdag clinic, do not necessarily humiliate people, but they are capable of doing so.*

With this core statement we not only had a positive ideal on the horizon as a focus point, but the board and staff felt a clear call: eliminate humiliating situations! This powerful statement thickened the outlines of our humanisation ideal and provided points of reference for policy and for our attitude towards the inmates.

Critical opposition: Foucault

Next to the sources mentioned above we delved into Habermas' (1981) discussion of the dilemmas of the balance between the world of *systems* of organisations and the *lifeworld* of people. However, for critical self-reflection we especially invoked help from the works of Michel Foucault. His anti-humanist attitude in *The Birth of the Clinic* (2001), specifically dealing with power, discipline and control in institutions such as our psychiatric clinic, offered radical opposition. Foucault contends public institutions and prisons especially are part of a controlling power structure that serves to regulate and control populations. He opposes the prison itself as an institution, the political system and the system of justice, and anyone involved, such as scientists, social workers, therapists and psychiatrists. Any attempt at humanising such an institution is suspicious. Humanisation within a power structure cannot be anything but a tool reinforcing and legitimating this power itself, humanisation becoming a means to achieve political goals. A prison always remains primarily a part of a disciplinary structure that subjects people to its power (Foucault, 2001, p. 425–427).

This theory helped us to confront ourselves with critical questions. When were we really 'humanising' ourselves, more than actually caring for the organisation and its patients? I remember one meeting where I was exceptionally tired of the crisis and the workload, where I held an 'emphatic speech' about the necessity of cultural change, at some point saying that: '[…] whoever is not willing to go along should start looking for a new job'. Carefully, some dropped the name of Foucault. Suddenly I saw myself, the idealist, the man of horizontal management, communicating and directing vertically. I later apologised for this 'vertical' behaviour, which was incongruent with my own and our shared vision of horizontal management and dialogue.

Besides the ideal of a respectful and human-centred organisation stated in the positioning statement, we thus found guidance in multiple theoretical and philosophical sources. These sources not only reinforced us in our ambition – they critically questioned us along the way as well. The example just described shows how easily one can become misguided and lost in power positions – not because of evil will, but because one becomes blinded by good intentions. Evil, as Arendt (1963) stated, can be most banal. Managers intending to work on humanisation must be willing to reflect on themselves. Also, I hope to have shown, the space for reflection can be created and made part of the organisation and management processes, even in the midst of crisis – especially in the midst of crisis – by discussing shared sources of inspiration that also make it easier to confront each other.

Source: your own experience

During my first weeks in 1997 I was crossing the dark and closed halls of the clinic. I was in possession of an electronic key and wanted to open a door. The door blocked with a clicking sound; it would not open. A harsh voice coming from a loudspeaker instructed me. If I was walking with an inmate I could not open doors by myself. I could not see anyone; the voice was robotic and anonymous. I wondered who had such power to restrain me, a manager of this place, in my movement. It was alienating. I followed the instructions and moved aside so as to bring the inmate into full view of the camera. He had to state his name. After this I stated mine and I had to ensure the voice that everything was in order. The door opened.

This procedure repeated itself after about ten meters. And again, after ten meters, I tried to argue with the voice, that I had just done everything it asked, but it was unmovable; we were forced to repeat ourselves. The assembly line kept running, whatever we did. As we walked, the inmate and I had time to make some calculations. On an average day, when he would move around, he faced about eighty closed doors. For the seven years he had been here, every time he wanted or had to attend education or therapy, or went to the canteen for food or drinks or talks, he went through this procedure.

This experience inspired me – as manager and human being – to take action. In a phased process we implemented an open-door policy. Twenty-five doors were opened permanently. The freedom and the opportunity for self-organisation of the inmates increased, as did the mobility of staff. The security around the building functioned very well, so in our opinion safety was not endangered, while the atmosphere inside the clinic opened up. Because of the open doors it was suddenly more striking how boring and dull the halls were. Inmates and staff proposed projects to lighten the place up. An art commission was installed. Inmates worked with art students, using a reasonable budget to select art and furniture to create meeting places, corners to hang out and to give the place a fresh look. The atmosphere really changed with the open doors from grim to somewhat more colourful and open. This diminished the alienation felt regarding the building and the organisation as a whole. It became our building, not just an anonymous institution of the Department of Justice. A self-managed shop was opened, an Internet café initiated, the library had longer opening hours and last but not least, a few pets and aquaria with fish made the place more lively and hospitable.

In this way the place that these people lived in for years no longer emphasised the vertical structure of power and (anonymous) control through (digital) systems. There was more room for self-direction and the building was no longer a simple combination of prison and psychiatric clinic. It now had its own particular face to show and individual, meaningful character. By 1999 we started calling the incarcerated people 'patients', instead of stressing control by using the word 'inmate', again emphasizing a humane and safe treatment. Thus slowly the initiated change from control to treatment began to show itself in the organisation.

Conclusion

The ideals, the sources and the means described above just outline one of the many possibilities for setting course on the route to humanising an organisation. Historically humanisation is most visible in the battle to leave behind what is inhumane. In our day such inhumanity may increase by rationalising organisations and organising vertically more than necessary, subjecting everyone involved more and more to rules and procedures. Public organisations always exert forms of power that entail a formal inequality and need to be structured vertically to some degree. They necessarily restrain autonomy and self-direction. Rational arguments can be made about manageability, control and safety during a crisis, to increase the inequality within such power structures. However, when such vertical exertion of formal power is no longer just an adaptation or compromise, but comes to denigrate and corrodes the identity of both staff and clients, alienation becomes very real.

Organisations should critically question the ways in which they restrain or support autonomy, self-direction and self-organisation of the people they manage. This process is about finding the right balance, providing the safety and orientation of clear boundaries, but enabling a horizontal perspective in which those involved find the space for participatory dialogue and self-direction. Discipline need not be solely imposed top down; one may engage with the capacities – the freedom – of all involved to reach a way of being together that is as good and humane as it can be within the formal restrictions and inequalities given in public organisations. An organisation needs both to strive for positive ideals and to pay attention to those places where humiliation occurs and can be diminished or abolished. I have found it of crucial relevance to choose shared sources of inspiration that enable and stimulate discussion about ideals and provide signposts for a critical evaluation of progress and choices. When we neglect to put humane values on the horizon as an orientation, this horizon is colonised by the dominant tendency to rationalise organisations more and more. Last but not least, to me as a manager it was crucial to develop sensibility and take my own experience seriously.

Note

1 In this chapter we reflect on Anthonio's experience as a manager. For the sake of readability it is written in the first person singular.

References

Anthonio G.G. (2006) *De Humanisering van een justitiële organisatie, menselijke waarden als richtlijn voor organisatieverandering*. Utrecht: University for Humanistic Studies.
Bonger, H. and Hoogervorst, J.R.H. (eds) (1989) *Dirck Volckertzoon Coornhert, dwars maar recht*. Zutphen: De Walburg Pers.
Chaplin, C. (Producer & Director) (1936) Modern Times [motion picture]. United States: United Artists/MK2 Editions/Janus Films/Criterion.
Foucault, M. (2001) *Discipline toezicht en straf; De geboorte van een gevangenis* [Surveiller et punir, Naissance de la prison] (trans. Vertalerscollectief). Groningen: Historische Uitgeverij.
Goffman, E. (1993) *De dramaturgie van het dagelijks leven* [The presentation of self in everyday life] (trans. J. Mordegaai). Utrecht: Bijleveld.
Goffman, E. (1977) *Totale instituties* [Total institutions] (trans. E.D. de Jong – de Jonge). Rotterdam: Universitaire Pers.
Habermas, J. (1981) *Theorie des kommunikatieven Handelns: Band 1 & 2*. Frankfurt am Mein: Suhrkamp.
Hart, W. (2013) *Verdraaide organisaties. Terug naar de bedoeling*. Deventer: Vakmedianet.
Huijer, M. (2013) *Discipline: Overleven in overvloed*. Amsterdam: Boom.
Jansen T., van den Brink G. and Kole J. (eds) (2009). *Beroepstrots, Een ongekende kracht*. Amsterdam: Boom uitgeverij.
Kolind, L. and Botter, J. (2014) *Unboss*. Deventer: Vakmedianet.
Lissenberg, E., Swaaningen, R. van and Ruller, S. van (2001) *Tegen de regels IV, inleiding in de criminologie*. Nijmegen: Juridische uitgeverij Ars Aequi.
Ludwig, H. and Blom, R. (2001) *Onder dwang, het leven in een TBS-Inrichting*. Amsterdam/Antwerpen: Uitgeverij Veen.
Margalit, A. (1998) *The decent society*. Boston: Harvard University Press.
Nussbaum, M.C., (1997), *Cultivating humanity: A classical defense of reform in liberal education*. Harvard University Press: London.
Ossewaarde, R. (2006) *Maatschappelijke organisaties, een sociologische inleiding*. Amsterdam: Boom Onderwijs.
Peters J. and Pouw J. (2004) *Intensieve menshouderij. Hoe kwaliteit oplost in rationaliteit*. Schiedam: Scriptum.

Scharmer, C. O. (2013) *Theory U: Leading from the future as it emerges. The social technology of presencing*. San Francisco: Berrett-Koehler Publishers.

Scharmer O. and Kaufer K. (2013) *Leiden vanuit de toekomst. Van ego-systeem naar eco-systeem*. Zeist: Christofoor.

Verbrugge, A. (2005) 'Het procesdenken van managers berooft de wereld van zijn bezieling'. *NRC Handelsblad*, 18-06-05.

7 Humanisation in the advertising industry

Veronica Millan Caceres

> 'It is fate ... that sets the range of our available and realistic options, but ... that it is our character that selects among the options.' – Zygmunt Bauman (2000)

Introduction

Our multifaceted review of humanisation now continues with a review of how people in one particular industry – the advertising industry – manage the process of humanisation in the workplace. In particular, this chapter will touch upon the humanity that exists in this industry and how it is captured in the work environment of the contemporary digital age. I will examine[1] how the transformation in our means of communication has changed the advertising industry and society in different ways, the most unexpected of which is the blurring of the line between an employee's professional life and personal life. Social media and the technologies around it have changed the workplace environment – this change is often fraught with insecurities and doubts in the people that first begin to grapple with it. I will demonstrate how the personal becomes critical for the professional in the advertising industry in the context of these new technologies. The advertising industry is often seen as a barometer for other companies and industries because advertising agencies are chasing the latest trends to anticipate what society, as a whole, will experience.

Finally, through auto-ethnographic sketches of my real-world struggles with technology and humanisation within an advertising company, I would like to show how these forces are affecting the people inside the company and how the separation of the professional and personal life is changing. Seeing this dynamic through the lens of *liquid modernity* and humanisation gives keen insight as to how such forces may be playing out in other industries as well.

Understanding the advertising industry

Advertising is still a popular field in which many university graduates and artistically minded people want to work. Yet many people join the industry without understanding the true nature of the agencies. There are primarily two pressures that affect the industry: (1) the desire to be the pulse of society, to understand people, to find new ways to attract people to products or services for their clients and (2) the corporate need to be part of a publicly traded company, which carries with it the financial metrics and goals that shareholders and analysts expect from the holding company or the client (who is generally also a publicly traded company). These two often conflicting pressures bring about a certain chaos to the environment of the agency. Adding to the uncertainty there is a pressure to keep up with new technologies that have both changed the technical challenges of the job and the ways employees can relate to each other.

Unlike manufacturing companies, advertising agencies seek to understand society, demographics and people in order to produce advertising that will work for their target audience. The belief system in most advertising agencies is that they need to relate to society, to people, to be inspired and to keep their creativity. They do not see themselves as part of a *financialised* organisation that is worried about stock price or profit margin. This belief even shapes how the agencies are named – they are an advertising *agency*, not an advertising *corporation*. The industry does not use the term *corporation* although nowadays agencies are all corporations and for the most part, part of a holding company that is publically traded on one of the world's public stock exchanges. With this separation in name there is already a tension between the agencies and the holding companies. This tension arises because the advertising agencies see themselves in the business of people; they cater to their clients, serving a strategic or artistic purpose for society, rather than pursuing mere profits for stockholders. Many agencies owned by these holding companies will act as though they are not affiliated with their holding company masters. To advertising agencies the influence of the corporation is dehumanising, robbing them of their creativity; without creativity they cannot function or do their work for their clients.

The tension exists even within the agencies' client base. As client companies now turn more and more to their procurement departments to determine whether or not an ad agency is acceptable, many agencies (and even some of the client management) will complain that they no longer have the freedom to create interesting commercials or campaigns. The worth of an ad agency increasingly is measured by the clients' procurement departments using metrics around due diligence and, nowadays, primarily the bottom line cost. Thus, the clients' procurement apparatuses have eliminated the ad budgets needed for what is considered quality work within the agency. Agency management then have to make decisions about how much of a clients' budget can be used for higher quality work versus the profit margin demanded by the holding company, which is demanding positive quarterly results for their next shareholders' meeting. But more than that, the agencies have to make decisions about what is considered quality work, how to attract talented employees and how to retain the talent.

As technology has advanced and new forms of communication are being created, a new level of chaos and uncertainty is being added to the advertising industry. The Internet has created new digital lines of advertising services that are disrupting the industry, causing more changes and turmoil. Digital technologies have also changed the skills needed in the agencies (so they can survive) and have also changed society as a whole (how we communicate and interact). These changes have been brought into the advertising industry from two directions. First, the industry must understand the changes in society to find new ways to create services for clients that do not know how to navigate the new technologies. Second, people inside the agencies interacting with each other bring change that mirrors how society in general is now interacting.

Many employees do not survive the uncertainty of the advertising industry and leave tosomething less rocky, something calmer. For those that do manage to thrive in the industry and who end up in management, they understand that the relationships and the humanisation of the agency are critical to making people (talent) stay in order to do the work. Without these talented humans to do the work, the actual services to the client would be impossible.

Academics, philosophers, organisational experts, sociologists and many others have noted these changes in society and in the workplace and have introduced many theories as to how organisations will be affected by, and may or may not adapt to, such change. One particular theory that may provide special understanding for those executives, managers, human resources personnel and others trying to cope with this dynamic world is the theory of *liquid modernity*.

Liquid modernity and advertising

Liquid modernity, a theory that Polish-born sociologist Zygmunt Bauman has been developing since the late 1980s, tries to create an understanding of where our society is today. Modernity is the cultural tendency to rationalise processes in order to increase control and predictability and secure the progress of human civilisation. This results in (technically) solidifying organisations. The organisational form par excellence of modernity is bureaucracy. However, in Bauman's analyses, this is a process that undermines itself.

Bauman's book, *Modernity and the Holocaust* (1989), for example, is a radical understanding of how a 1920–30s German government, presumably comprised of rational beings, experienced a dehumanisation of the organisation that ultimately led to thousands of German citizens and bureaucrats making decisions that precipitated the demise of millions. The 'dehumanisation' that Bauman identifies is born from Western civilisation's desire to 'dominate' over 'barbarism, reason against ignorance, objectivity against prejudice, progress against degeneration, truth against superstition …' (Bauman, 1989). The Holocaust defined for Bauman what modernity could (and did) become: a (bureaucratic) process-focused society without room for human intervention. Thus according to Bauman the process of modernity was really cyclical. Organisations, systems, roles, businesses etc. become solidified according to certain ideals but in the end this solidification is what undermines the original ideals. Then we start a new to rebuild structures to capture (new) ideals. Modernity tears down a process and rebuilds it.

In his seminal work *Liquid Modernity*, Bauman posits that changes in society over the last two centuries – beginning with the emergence of the industrial revolution and its transformative effect on all aspects of society – have resulted in a new type of 'modernity'. This is an iterative process that seems to be speeding up, as technologies were further developed further to make factories more efficient, accounting and finance more precise and workers more efficient. Because the speed of this process of tearing down and rebuilding was increasing, what seemed to be a certain or a solid environment now seemed more liquid, like water flowing.

This process of changing and removing the old for the new, aptly named *liquid modernity*, has created an increasingly faster cycle, causing solid, hierarchical structures to come down and be reborn in a liquefying process. If technology is allowing society to compress time and space, according to Bauman's theory, then change is happening at faster speeds. The Industrial Revolution and its results are defined by Bauman as the solid part of modernity because of the structure it created in the factories that were built – specific roles for workers, monolithic management, and assembly line production. Yet while more and more products could be produced, a complimentary aspect of these factories and their prodigious manufacturing was lacking: the products had to be sold. New and better-fitting markets had to be created to foster the demand for these goods. The market needed to be liquefied in order to sell the abundance of products. Mass-market advertising, consequently, came into being and came of age. The liquidity of the advertising industry, therefore, can be associated with its origins (Millan Caceres, 2014).

Bauman also believes that liquid modernity and technology have effectively inverted the traditional model of Foucault's *Panopticon* in the workplace. First designed by English philosopher and social theorist Jeremy Bentham in the 1780s, the *Panopticon* was an institutional building – like a prison – in which a single watchman could observe all of the inmates with the inmates being aware that they could be watched at all times but unable to see the actual watchman. Almost two hundred years later, French philosopher Michel Foucault used the *Panopticon* as a metaphor for disciplinary societies that tend to observe and attempt to normalise human behaviour. Now in liquid modernity, Bauman inverts Foucault's *Panopticon* such that, rather than managers and supervisors watching over (solid modernity) factory workers, it is the liquid modernity workers that watch and see the spectacle in front of them through these new digital technologies we now call 'social media'. This is what Thomas Mathiesen called in *The Viewer Society* a *Synopticon*, in which 'the many see the few' (Mathiesen, 1997).

Ad agencies, who benefited from technology through the creation of new mediums or because services could be rendered faster and cheaper (a billboard could go up faster with improvements in printing, for example), now also had to deal with the compression of time and space in the organisation. Clients want faster delivery of projects, for less cost, in diverse markets. Agencies had to face new technologies that forced faster response, if the agency was dealing in real time with consumers. These constant challenges added to the liquidity of the environment and have prevented agencies from becoming staid and bland – agencies have to be open, adaptable, and creative to continue to attract clients and attract employees that could deliver for those clients.

For holding companies, this flexibility that the advertising agencies present creates a tension. The holding companies still represent the most solid aspect of how agencies function. Corporate holding companies own approximately 85 per cent of the agencies around the world. By and large, they are focused on the bottom line, on making sure that stock analysts' predictions of margins and growth are met or exceeded. The holding companies care about efficiencies, economies of scale, control and predictability. This is often contrary to desires of the agencies' management. While the management at an advertising agency understands the 'solid modern' requirements of a holding company's shareholders, they have to manage the 'liquid modern' industry and the people (employees, clients and consumers) that are in it. Liquid modernity, in the case of the advertising industry, breaks apart solid structures that would otherwise bring bureaucracy into the advertising agencies, creating a tension between the two organisations.

To elaborate this tension between structure and liquidity in the industry would require a book in and of itself. For the purposes of this chapter I will now turn to the role of technology within ad agencies as a work environment.

Technology, liquidity and the advertising agency

Technology's role in the increasing liquefaction of society and industry is of a particular interest in the already liquid industry of advertising. The Web and social media have enhanced the ad industry itself by improving the technical quality of advertisements and reducing costs (as technology became cheaper). Now, the advent of the 'digital world', with its mobile devices of all kinds, wearable devices, different operating systems, and the different applications that run on these systems, is further challenging the ad industry. Agencies are coming to understand the possibility of advertising not in the traditional context of a print advertisement or a television commercial, but through the development of an iPhone Operating System application (iOS app) or a game that is also an advertisement. In order to do all of this, the agencies have to be able to understand consumer behaviour, to understand the 'human' and what they both want and need, as a means of targeting their behaviour to be able to sell a product or create brand loyalty.

Here, the context of Bauman's inverse *Panopticon* takes on an interesting perspective, since advertising has embraced technology for its own benefit, but also for that of its clients, towards the goal of selling the brand or product to consumers. Whereas before, brand managers had to chase after an audience (*Panopticon*), digital technologies now have brought consumers (audiences) to them. Today's consumer has no qualms in expecting to have an interaction with brands immediately (*Synopticon*). The audience is now talking back and the companies that make these products have to be prepared for this conversation. Many of them outsource this conversation to advertising agencies. This fits nicely with the digital campaigns that many of these agencies are already doing for their clients, and the successful ones have been able to give a personality to a brand, to create the 'conversation' that consumers today demand.

As much as technology has transformed these markets, advertising is still focused on the relationship that a human being (a potential consumer) has with the commodity that is being sold. Managing that relationship is what the advertising agency is hired to do: to create a relationship between the consumer and the commodity through, for example, company or brand awareness campaigns, and ultimately to 'close' the relationship by convincing the consumer to embrace the company, purchase the product, or use the service. Because the act of advertising is based on human relationship and knowledge, humanisation is invariably part of the process. The agency creating the branding, or the product packaging, or the glossy print, or the website for the client, has to engage in the process of understanding the other, the other who will buy the product or the experience or the feeling. While automation and technology have attempted to routinise some of the aspects of the process, there is still much that cannot be converted into algorithms and lines of computer code.

That ad work itself is based on understanding and fostering human relationships helps in creating a human-focused work environment (for example, through flexible work hours, flexible work locations, and free events to promote employee unity). The socialisation of the advertising employee happens at all levels of the organisation, not only at the highest levels (the 'old boys' network') or at the lower levels ('newbies' sticking together); it is part of the requirement for selling the services to the client. In the end, agencies are selling a service, not a physical product, so the relationship fostered with clients is critical. This socialisation then is taken into the agency itself, as part of the culture of the industry, perpetuating the humanising treatment of the worker.

However, these connections between employees in the ad agencies are combining with the advent of the digital world to blur the distinction between personal and professional. Reaching a consumer through a digital platform, for example, is as effective as doing a direct marketing campaign or presenting a television ad. Many workers bring their digital technology skills from their personal life to their work life. The question is, whether or not this is still a humanising trend.

Online relationships: public and private life within an ad agency

The digital technology revolution of the last fifteen years has transformed the way we consider and tend to our interpersonal relationships. In liquid modernity, Bauman has a concern that by digitising our relationships, we are less likely to be engaged with one another. Digital relationships 'are "virtual relationships"' and 'unlike "real relationships", "virtual relationships" are easy to enter and to exit' (Bauman, 2003). This supports the liquidity of relationships and ultimately, according to Bauman, reduces our responsibility to the other. However, recent studies have shown that interactive online relationships have become the norm and despite the 'virtuality' of the relationship, affect the participants as though they were 'real relationships' (Delistraty, 2014). The changing way that we interact with each other now makes even the distinction between an 'online' friendship or a 'real' one an antiquated view of relationships.

And this understanding of, and apparent indifference to, the differences between online and real relationships is critical to the success of many new employees in advertising agencies. Clients are requesting better interaction with their consumers online, not only to sell their products, but to maintain their brands and reputation. Agencies exclusively dedicated to social media public relationships have been increasing in number in order for the brands (clients) that hired them to 'embrace online communities a way to directly connect with people as human beings' (Proulx, 2015).

Because of this blurring between online and real, work and personal lives can easily coexist in ad agencies. Employees are allowed (and often encouraged) to use their skills in social media for their clients and show off those skills through their own personal accounts. Personal interaction is not relegated to water-cooler conversations; instead such interaction is more likely to be about personal details – a weekend party at someone's house, the resulting headache the next morning – all in front of other co-workers and even management. The result is that these relationships will then include connecting on social media platforms, where the details of these personal events, parties, outings or vacations (and more) are readily accessible to the co-worker or their manager. What was traditionally the manager overseeing the workers can now be flipped to include the workers seeing the manager in their personal life through social media (*Synopticon*). It is now the norm in the agency world to interact with your co-workers through social media.

As an employee in the advertising industry, there is a certain anxiety in allowing my co-workers to enter my personal life. Yet contrary to what Bauman contends, these personal connections have the distinct possibility of humanising the other, as you now are aware of your co-worker's personal life and this ends up building a relationship that may not have happened if the only interactions that occurred between you were in person in the workplace.

Working in advertising in a digital world

From day one of my career with the advertising agency, the face-to-face socialisation was alarming enough, especially coming from a financial services background in which there was a clear separation of my personal self from my work self. I quickly learned, however, that such communal social interactions promoted team building and gave me the opportunity for off-the-record conversations to ask for help or support in the projects I needed to complete. I began to understand that this type of personal–work interaction was normal for my company and, later, normal for the industry itself.

My initial discomfort for the blurred line between my personal and professional life was not limited to face-to-face communications – they turned to online interactions too. At first, most of the requests for connection were coming on social media platforms geared toward professional relationships like Plaxo or LinkedIn, which made perfect sense. I could understand the desire to create networking opportunities of this kind. Because social media was still new, and not many of my personal, non-work friends were on it, these initial interactions were a bit awkward, but maintaining an online list of professional contacts was more efficient than keeping an ever-growing number of business cards in a desk drawer.

When online requests from co-workers to be a 'friend' or a 'follower' started to arrive from various other social media platforms, I was even less prepared. These same contacts from career-oriented social media sites were sending friend requests on personal social media sites like Facebook, and eventually, there were requests to 'follow' on Twitter or Instagram, as new platforms were created. And the tacit pressure to accept all of these requests was palpable. On conference calls there would be idle talk about people who were not on Facebook or allowing access to social media sites, as if someone's desire to protect their personal space was something that had to be explained rather than simply understood. Within weeks of starting my job in the advertising industry, the trickle of access requests turned into a tide – more and more requests from co-workers, whether I knew them well from working on a project together or whether they just knew of me, to add them to my personal social media sites.

Despite my initial hesitation, I eventually accepted these requests for these professional contacts to enter my private world. I often wondered what the limits of my relationships with these people were (or should be). Back then, I gave scant thought to those considerations that today are fodder for the evening news; I blithely disregarded privacy concerns and thoughts of how these social media platforms were using my personal data. (Ironically, most sites were selling my own data right back to advertising agencies affiliated with my own company.) Instead, my main concern was whether I was going to present aspects of my personal life online that could, perhaps, become detrimental to my professional life. This was especially true when I received a friend request on my private Facebook page from my manager at the time. I became worried that the places I visited, the things I did, and the words I wrote in my personal space would somehow negatively affect her perceptions of me (and potentially, hinder my career advancement).

As the first year or so of my tenure in the advertising industry passed, the adoption of social media in our society grew as more and more people joined the platforms to get in touch with old school friends, interact with family members in remote places, or benignly stalk that certain ex. Thus, I found myself connecting through social media with many more friends and family. This made my conundrum even more acute: did I really want to mix my personal and private lives on these social media platforms? This anxiety often spilled over into the 'real life' interactions with my co-workers. Pictures from events or meetings were uploaded to social media platforms. I often wondered whether this affected people's behaviour at these events – knowing that they were being 'documented' for posting online; I know that it made me more hesitant to really be free. I longed for the sense of privacy that the pre-social media world gave to your social interactions.

What I realised was that it was only some of us that fretted over the pictures and the mixing of the worlds – certain personality types were more open and had no issues with their personal and professional lives mixing together. I also found that the comfort or discomfort of the mixing of personal and professional lives was not a function of age.

There is a tendency to assume that the younger generations are more adaptable to social media than the older ones; however, this was not necessarily the case in my environment. Young or old, 'techie' or 'creative', British or American, whether it was extremist political views or adorable pictures of their children, there were co-workers who had no issues sharing the intimate details of their life, pictures of their drinking games on a Friday night, or their personal philosophies.

Social media and advertising

Interestingly, the driver for many of the online interactions as described above was the ad agency itself. We were being asked to learn about these digital platforms so we could understand the new direction of the business. Advertising agencies were aggressively using social media platforms with the goal of presenting their ability to navigate social media, as a sales point for their clients and as a means of attraction and retention of employees. Social media managers promoted employees' activities in social media to promote the agency, to make it look more popular. The expectation, of course, is that we are using our own personal social media accounts to follow, support or promote our company's agenda. We all knew to beware of the Social Media Analyst, Manager, or Coordinator that you were interacting with at a corporate event or a social event designed by the agency: your picture may end up on your agency's Twitter account or Facebook page! The blurring of the personal and the professional continues ...

Of course, posting about professional themes or showing yourself online to be an expert in specific areas can result in more connections and those can eventually lead to job opportunities. Yet this volatile mixture of the personal and the professional is not without risk. Notorious cases in the United States in the last few years have included the story of public relations executive Justine Sacco, who prior to boarding a plane for a family vacation posted a tweet that was understood to be offensive (rather than funny). By the time she landed at her destination, she had been publically shamed for her comment. Within days, her employer fired her because of the digital circus that unfolded in her personal (but public) online life (Stelter, 2015).

Because social media platforms have become so ubiquitous and integrated to our social life through 'free' use, the necessity to create revenue streams from advertising (rather than charging for the social media platform) was inevitable. Most social media platforms became new outlets for advertising and became a means to reach out to the consumer in a non-traditional manner. Today, advertising agencies (in large part digital shops) are creating new social media platforms themselves (for example, Huge Inc. developed an application called 'Honey') as the line between digital advertising and technology companies is blurring.

As an advertising industry employee, my social media world has transformed into an advertising platform for my company. My Facebook, LinkedIn, Instagram and Twitter accounts are now littered with current and former co-workers and I follow my agencies online. My online social interactions with these people maintain the connections we may have created face to face (or we are creating a connection with no actual interaction in person). There is now less doubt and anxiety around accepting a professional contact on my personal social media. I have come to focus more on how I can use social media to better my professional standing; I am no longer obsessed with trying to control my privacy and separate my social and family world from my professional one. It is an open question whether (or how long) users of these social media platforms will continue to use what have essentially become advertising platforms, but for now, the blurring of the personal and professional is complete.

The question that has been answered for me, personally, after being in the advertising industry for almost a decade, is that social and personal interactions are not just the norms of the advertising agency, but requirements for the industry. There is an integral part of humanity that is required to be expressed and developed in order to be in an advertising agency and to thrive there professionally. The agency needs to know humans: it needs to entice humans to work within it; it needs to express its humanity as a means to attract clients; and, ultimately, it needs to be managed by humans. The humanisation of the corporate environment in the advertising industry is what allows advertising to be understanding of the human psyche to motivate someone to become a consumer.

But fundamentally, for the person living the liquidity of the industry, having to deal with the changing environment – technological or otherwise – the close relationships that are developed help us navigate the uncertainty of the industry. The technological aspects that have invaded the industry, through social media or whatever comes next, is but the means through which we develop the relationships that will help us carry on.

Conclusion: what comes next?

What could we extrapolate from these ideas of liquid modernity, the advertising industry, and the humanisation that we see in this industry?

The advertising industry can be a bellwether for what other industries will see in their own environments if their relationships with consumers are as important as in the ad industry. Management in these industries has to take heed on what liquidity will do to their organisation; rapid changes, uncertainty, and new coping mechanisms are necessary to manage the liquidity. The advertising industry is proposing an interesting tactic to manage the uncertainty and chaos: the humanisation of the management of the organisation. In the ad industry, instead of bureaucratisation, employees and management manage the liquid environment by creating flexible, human-based policies and work environments. As liquidity takes over, it is human relationship development that will help companies survive.

Technology is also changing the way companies interact with their customers. If advertising agencies are helping companies understand their consumer and better serve them, these client companies also have to recognise their own responsibility in providing that information to their own marketing departments (or their outside advertising agency). It is no longer acceptable to be silent and not communicate with your customer. In this digital, connected age, companies must interact with the consumer. It is critical to maintain a brand, and to keep sales going. Through today's social media an unsatisfied customer can easily find other unsatisfied customers that are willing to create a boycott or a public relations nightmare for that company or product. Therefore, it is also critical for companies to have people who can relate to customers, create the dialog, and serve them better. While fifty years ago it may have been enough for a company to thrive to just produce a good product, today's consumer wants a relationship with a company as well as its products and brands.

There are three critical points for management to give attention to. As Bauman has said, liquidity is about rapid changes and reversals. The humanisation of the way the ad agencies are managed can flip into its opposite in three ways.

First, if the personal and the professional are thoroughly mixed, the organisation can become a *Panopticon*, watching everything an employee does. When this happens, authentic interactions and actions on social media become problematic. This happens when, as I described, people are afraid that their personal opinions may negatively affect their professional chances. Agencies and companies need to give clarity to employees about this.

Second, organisations need to protect their employees because of the mixing of customers, employees and companies online – both to attract and retain employees and to enable social media to remain platforms where people feel free to speak. Sacco (like others) made a statement publicly but on a personal account, and the working of the *Synopticon* backfired when her company fired her because of public opinion about her personal statements. Because employees will often say in their social media posts *where* they work, a customer may see these employees as representing their companies even when the employees are not specifically empowered to do so. Therefore, companies need to consider adopting policies to define what it means for employees to speak on behalf of their company, their product, or their brand. These policies are critical, because even when employees know that they are not representing their company in a discussion, the association is implicit. Organisations need to understand this direct, social media link between their employees and their private and public network.

Third, technologies will change again. The ways to interact with customers through social media are incorporated into companies. It is paramount to take care that this is not taken as some kind of new certainty. Once these interactions become stabilised, the authenticity in the interactions may dissolve into bureaucratized information flows.

Zygmunt Bauman and others voiced a concern that liquid modernity erodes personal relationships – by digitising our interactions, we are less likely to be engaged with one another. I contend that liquidity (with all its uncertainties and decimation of solid structures) is an opportunity for us to interact with one another to better understand each other. There is always a risk that the humanising potential is lost. But the liquidity of an environment like the advertising industry today gives us a chance, as we survive the chaos, to find ways to relate to one another that can bring us closer. The industry gives people a chance to focus on other people, as consumers, but as humans, too.

Note

1 For parts of this chapter I draw on Millan Caceres, V. (2014) *Liquid persuaders*.

References

Bauman, Z. (2000) *Liquid modernity*. Cambridge: Polity Press.
— (2003) *Liquid love: On the frailty of human bonds*. Cambridge: Polity.
— (1989) *Modernity and the Holocaust*. New York: Cornell University Press.
Delistraty, C.C. (2014) 'Online relationships are real', *The Atlantic* (online), October 2, 2014. Retrieved April 3, 2015. www.theatlantic.com/health/archive/2014/10/online-relationships-are-real/380304/.
Mathiesen, T. (1997) 'The viewer society: Michel Foucault's "Panopticon" revisited', *Theoretical Criminology: An International Journal* 1 (2), p. 215–32.
Millan Caceres, V. (2014) *Liquid persuaders: The advertising holding company in the age of liquidity*.
Proulx, M. (2015) 'There is no more social media – just advertising: Five strategies for brands in the era of #notreally social media marketing', *Advertising Age* (online), April 2, 2015. Retrieved April 3, 2015. http://adage.com/article/digitalnext/social-media-advertising/297841/.
Stelter, B. (2015) '"Ashamed": Ex-PR exec Justine Sacco apologizes for AIDS in Africa Tweet', *CNN Online* (online), December 22, 2013. Retrieved April 3, 2015. www.cnn.com/2013/12/22/world/sacco-offensive-tweet/.

8 Discourse and humanisation in health care organisations

Clóvis Ricardo Montenegro de Lima

Introduction

This chapter describes my development as a professional in health organisations, initially as a physician and later as an administrator. This development started with uneasiness and feelings of powerlessness during the rise of the HIV/AIDS epidemic in the middle eighties in Brazil. My observations of the management of this epidemic made me question the human and social dimension of medical work. I came to understand the limitations of individual physicians and started to see medicine as a social practice that requires critical social approaches for problems of health and disease in societies, especially in unequal societies.

In the 1990s I was dedicated primarily to professional work as an administrator of health organisations, mainly working in public health services. During this time I studied Business Administration and Information Science. One of the perspectives that helped me develop a perspective on a more humane organisation of health care is that of Jurgen Habermas, whom I met when he visited Brazil to launch the translation of his book *Moral Consciousness and Communicative Action* (1990). At that same time I had the opportunity to take a course on his work with his translator for Portuguese, Flavio Beno Siebeneichler. This course showed me the possibilities of a philosophy of language in its pragmatic approach. It was a profound turning point in my understanding of reality, giving rise to the material reality of interactions mediated by language. The simultaneity of working and studying made me have a better relationship between theory and practice. I always try to improve my theories, and always submit my action to theoretical criticism. This relationship between theory and practice debugs things that I study, while it induces an action sharply criticised in my professional work.

Habermas (1987) taught us about the co-origin between subjectivity and intersubjectivity, which means that I cannot learn without interacting with the other, and I cannot do things better without learning. To be a human subject we need to communicate – dehumanisation occurs when people are isolated from rational communication with others. To understand the other's place in the formation of intersubjectivity, and to understand the place of intersubjectivity in the formation of subjectivity, has profound consequences for the management of organisations. The administrator who understands the place of the other leaves the observer's perspective, and takes the perspective of participants in organisations. With Habermas' theory of communicative action we can conceptualize (administrative) systems as part of the living world. Speech and communication become relevant ethical actions. Communication processes are no longer just an issue of effectiveness; they pose ethical questions that have implications for the morality of the social group in organisations as a whole and society at large. This understanding by management requires a clear ethical choice by administrators, a willingness to interact and argue and to discuss the definition of practical arrangements. In this chapter we will show how this works in practice.

Finally, we highlight the importance of a critique in light of effectiveness in organisations. It is important to understand how organisations necessarily reduce their internal complexity, in relation to their surroundings. Luhmann (1984) highlights how a system is fundamentally different from its environment. It is built on choices that serve the realisation and reproduction of certain goals. It should be noted that this reduction is not made for moral reasons, but for pragmatic and ideological reasons. Written or spoken communicative interactions are replaced by structured information flows in light of such goals. The tendency to reduce complexity has profound consequences for the possibility for humanisation in organisations. To opt for discussions with users and participants about problems in the organisations is going against the process of reducing the complexity that originated them. How to reconcile the need for complexity reduction with the perspective of communicative action?

Medicine, bureaucracy and human dimension of health care

In talking about the birth of social medicine, Michel Foucault (1973) argues that medicine is always social, and only in the relationship between the medical doctor and the patient does it have some individual characteristics. He said that medicine is part of a political strategy to control individual bodies and the bodies of governments. Thus, medicine is also an exercise of power that disseminates in a society, mediating the relationship of people with their own body and the bodies of others.

Working as a doctor specialising in infectious diseases in the city of São Paulo in the mid-80s, when the HIV/AIDS epidemic was emerging, it was not hard to understand this dimension of the exercise of power in medicine. It had to do with (1) the very nature of infectious diseases, transmitted from one person to another within society, (2) the scientific, moral and political conflicts around epidemiological surveillance of this disease, and (3) the questions AIDS raised about habits related to blood and sex, whereby the HIV flowed socially.

HIV/AIDS put the loaded theme of sex in the centre of the debates of society. Something so deeply intimate and personal started to be part of the agenda of public reasoning. Early on AIDS was grossly used as an instrument against freedom of sexual orientation, as if HIV transmission were associated with the preferred sex partner and not having multiple partners. Later AIDS became the centre of a gigantic effort of ordering sexual action by scientific models. It was the main reason for controlling sexual behaviour in society.

Medicine as an institution produces a fragile line between care and power based on fear of death. This fear was used to make people behave *correctly*. If you act properly, you are protected from HIV and AIDS. Gradually this speech became more sophisticated, and soon became self-induced so that people themselves disciplined each other.

Communication and information sharing within the society were extremely important in the dynamic processes of operational and organisational change in dealing with the epidemic. In a sense, one can say that the epidemic of HIV/AIDS produced another epidemic: the epidemic of information. The ethical question of ownership of medical information emerged with great force after the HIV/AIDS epidemic. Information about the condition of a person with HIV or an AIDS patient became relevant because of the high lethality and therefore risk of the disease. In its early years it constituted a threat that social groups, enterprises and governments wanted to avoid. Knowing if someone was sick or a carrier was an instrument to prevent losses. The control of this information became a powerful tool of social control, for inclusion or exclusion (Lima, 2005). Selective dissemination of information is part of the medical strategy and bio-political control.

The height of the dehumanisation of health organisations during the AIDS epidemic was the total isolation and denial of care for people with the disease. Despite the high mortality of the disease, which required hospital care and intensive care units, there were many cases in which organisations and health professionals refused to serve the needy. This refusal was intertwined with the denial of the very *raison d'être* of these organisations. Some health officials even suggested the social exclusion of people with AIDS, reproducing the classic medical model of leprosy control.

The victims of HIV/AIDS produced their own speech. Initially it was a defensive speech, which sought to highlight their role as victims and not as the cause of this serious social issue. The victims of the epidemic disease defended their leading role in the struggle for life and health as a positive representation of welfare. People came together to protect privacy, confidentiality, right to information, anticipation of social benefits, access to procedures for lymphocyte count and viral load measurement, and access to antiretroviral therapy (Lima, 2005). Gradually this speech formed an agenda of social and human rights, and thereafter set up a body of moral and political interests. It was a discourse anchored strongly in defence of human dignity in its strict sense. Insofar as the epidemic progressed and differentiated, these speeches included new demands that expanded into the legal sphere.

The traditional medical rationalisation seemed not to respond to the human dimension of the HIV/AIDS epidemic. The proliferation of speeches in the public sphere implies the definition of methods to construct practical arrangements.

The AIDS epidemic showed me some things that remained opaque throughout medical training. First, I saw the strong content of bureaucratic rationalisation of life in medical professional action. As Foucault described, each small action of a medical doctor carries different content. Birth, eat, cry, grow, walk, interact, learn: everything is mediated by thousands of bureaucratic scientific models, interfering deeply in the human dimension of existence. The human dimension seems to be emptied and replaced by bureaucratic reason. Second, consciously or unconsciously, this rationality is seemingly driven by ideological motives. It was this issue that pushed me into a philosophical social science approach in medicine (Lima, 2005). However, with Foucault's perspective on power, there seems to be no solution to the proliferation of different rationalities that do not communicate and keep excluding each other. This conflict can also be understood as a contemporary version of what is called the struggle for cultural hegemony.

From the systems theory perspective of Niklas Luhmann, we can understand that in organisations a reduction is always necessary. This is what organisations do: they reduce the complexity and unpredictability of a problem into known and controllable processes. In this process during the epidemic, as shown above, medical organisations excluded the individual and human aspects of the problem of HIV/AIDS in order to manage it. For the patients, something crucial was lost – from their perspective, the problem was not managed well at all. However, we should not just replace this rationality by another: we must amplify their humanistic bases.

The issue that arose for me in pursuing a social science approach to medicine was: considering that medical technology is effective for solving some of the problems of individuals and society at large, it is necessary not only to organise the voice of victims of the HIV/AIDS epidemic to defend their interests, but also to rebuild the medical rationale in terms of broader interests than those established within the professional corporation itself. This reconstruction of medical rationality implies expanding the group of people involved in the debate to reorganise the assumptions, methods and applications they are involved with (Lima, 2005).

My perception of the social process of the epidemic presented two major problems: first, the epistemological question how to understand this dynamic, and second, the practical question of how to respond to ethical and political demands – how to reconstruct complexity rationally, given the necessary reductions that organisations make. In both cases it seemed that the communicative action and discourse theories of Habermas would be useful in seeking solutions. He was my starting point for the study of philosophy of language, especially his studies of a pragmatic approach (Habermas, 1990).

In epistemological terms the solution I found was to think of the problem like a language game. The accommodation of the interests in a humanistic rationality reconstructed by the actors can be thought of as a grammar of the way of life in pluralistic and democratic societies. The agreements do not involve a practice built to submit people to the same rationality, but simply to offer viewpoints and arguments that support them. I will now discuss two periods in the next decade, in which I tested these ideas.

Health policies in the public sphere

In the early nineties I was working in the city of Joinville, in southern Brazil. This urban centre of half a million inhabitants was created by German descendants and had more than a third of its population working in the metallurgical, mechanical and plastic industries. At that time I was making the professional transition from clinical medicine to administering health organisations. My concern became increasingly focused on the interaction of health organisations with society (Lima, 2007).

Working with outpatients in a public health centre on the outskirts of the city, I became aware of my inability to solve the major health problems of that small community. This anxiety was shared with other colleagues working in other public health centres. The social processes of health and disease were much stronger than our ability to intervene and solve problems in health centres. We concluded that it was poor health care for poor people.

Interestingly this city was trying to train medical students in a similar way as in the NHS service in England. This residence had functioned since the mid-80s, and faced great difficulties to survive. I was fortunate to be invited to work with the young medical residents, teaching courses in epidemiology and health services administration. It was extremely important to learn about the possibility of overcoming the fragmentation of medical work at the level of primary health care.

By focusing on the experiences of the outpatient in the periphery, and being in touch with teaching in general medicine, I began a dual dialogue of extreme importance. On the one hand, there was everyday talk with other health professionals who were dissatisfied with the results of their work. On the other hand, I was having meetings with organised sectors of local society, especially in the suburbs. These meetings involved associations in poor neighbourhoods and groups of pastoral health of the Catholic Church.

The conversations showed me the dynamics of exclusion of the poor in discussions about health policies in the city. It was extremely painful to realise how the 500 doctors working in the city were defending their corporate interests, formally in the form of a cooperative work. Most workers in local industries had private plans for health assistance. Thus, the public health system did not have much relevance to the formal economy of the city and remained working at a precarious level.

In this context we started working on two levels to change health policies in the city of Joinville. On one level, we started to gather the stories and understand the discourse of health professionals in one of the poorest neighbourhoods of the city, an occupied area of mangroves. On another level, we participate in a circuit of meetings and discussions with neighbourhood associations and pastoral groups on the need to change health policy as part of a strategy to defend human rights.

The discourse of health professionals resulted in an experimental project called 'Health Factory', which aimed to develop appropriate technologies for primary health care. Its main line of action was to use the discussion between different health professionals to define practical arrangements for common action beneficial for society at large, or the common good. This project was based on an agreement between two institutions of higher education in the city. Although we never got a formal agreement with the municipal government, we still achieved important results in concrete terms locally, and above all created evidence that public health centres could operate differently.

On another level we worked on the deployment of national health care in the city as part of a wider social dynamic. This health system was an innovation in social security in Brazil, determined in the Constitution of 1988, which was only regulated as law two years later. It was a joint effort by the local Centre for Defence of Human Rights, groups of pastoral health of the Catholic Church and a federation of associations of residents of Joinville. Later this cooperative effort included the membership of trade unions and associations of health professionals.

We can understand networks of interests as an effort to protect a point of view with good arguments. But with both the health professionals and the community leaders there were no protective actions and there was also no desire to critique the assumptions of any one of the participants of this broad alliance. By bringing the two perspectives into contact, they understood how they needed each other if they wanted to change the situation they were all dealing with. When the discussion broadened, the powerbase of the community grew with it (Lima, 2007).

This new association could now confront the city counsel, which eventually led to a change in the morality of the city counsel. The discussion around this morality resulted in a confrontation between two policies. On the one hand, there was an elitist policy, exclusionary, led by great entrepreneurs in association with a local conservative government. On the other, there was a democratic policy, inclusive, that emerges in poor neighbourhoods, but has the strength to win allies among the middle classes and health professionals.

The outcome of this confrontation was the regulation of the health system. It created permanent collegiate councils, with the participation of governments, service providers, health professionals and fifty percent of representatives of different user segments. The institutionalisation of those informal conversations between health professionals, community leaders and union leaders as a city health council became the major political confrontation in the city. The interventions of the public ministry to promote the diffuse collective interests were important for success in the creation of this health council (Lima, 2007).

In more abstract terms, this experience in Joinville showed that the perception of social relations as interactions mediated by language has methodological advantages. Thus, the conflict experience could be thought of at the same time as a ground for discussion to build understanding and practical arrangements. Breaking the monopoly of the specialist medical fraternity speech was very important for effective health policy discussion in the city. The incorporation of the speeches of other health professionals and the speech of the common people expanded the community of communication involved and required better arguments (Lima, 2007).

Another example: quality of care in health organisations

Niklas Luhmann (1984) teaches us that organisations are built from the reduction of complexity in relation to the environment. Thus, an organisation always chooses means for performing an aim among many possibilities. This reduction of complexity in organisations happens particularly by reducing the communication within it, with structuring information flows around the choices made. The rationalisation in organisations is always a choice, geared for some purpose, notably the imperatives of power and money (Carvalho and Lima, 2007; Lima et al., 2010).

A rational reconstruction of some the complexity of human affairs through discourse analysis implies that people in organisations can interact and communicate about more issues than what is initially defined. A problem is usually outlined through a reduction of the complexity involved in practice. This complexity reduction begins with the choice of means and continues with effective coordination of resources for their implementation. Do more, do better or do differently means increasing the complexity within organisations, increasing the number of interactions and communication among the people. Arguing is increasing the complexity of an organisation (Carvalho and Lima, 2009; Lima et al., 2010). Dialogue and using the Habermas outline on how to organise the right context for interaction helps in reorganising the issues, and in opening up to and rationally reconstructing this complexity.

In the middle nineties I worked in the planning division of the AIDS national program, reviewing the first operational plans from twenty-seven states and fifty priority municipalities. Our focus in this work was the integration of the program in the permanent actions of the National Health System, especially its inclusion among the activities of family health programs. This work was successful, and the Brazilian program became a world reference in the control of the HIV/AIDS epidemic.

Working in the national AIDS program and knowing the main problems, I decided to make my work my doctoral research topic in management. So I worked on the issue of the quality of health care organisations for persons with HIV/AIDS as a thesis. My assumption was that the focus of interest in quality between health professionals and their patients was not the same. I understood that health professionals were more interested in technical aspects and patients in interactional aspects and amenities, and, fortunately, I was wrong (Lima, 2005).

At the beginning of 1996 some medical researchers presented their first results relating to combined antiretroviral triple therapy. These results changed the entire strategy for health care of people with HIV/AIDS. This strategy was based on palliative care and psychosocial support and was focused on tests for lymphocyte count and viral load, and consequent access to medicines. The National Congress of Brazil approved a law guaranteeing free access to antiretroviral drugs. All this happened under the watchful eye of mobilised people with HIV/AIDS and their self-help groups.

In evaluating the deployment of triple antiretroviral therapy in Brazil, the seven pillars of quality defined by Avedis Donabedian (1980) were applied: efficacy, efficiency, effectiveness, acceptability, legitimacy, profitability and equity. Around these pillars we tried to argue with the protagonists of the social process: coordinators of the AIDS national program, state and local coordinators, health professionals and people with HIV/AIDS. This discussion allowed for the capturing of different viewpoints, and the building of a narrative that allows us to understand what happened.

In this context I was working with a group that tested the first design of the new hospital accreditation method in Brazil. This testing was sponsored by the Pan American Health Organisation (PAHO). We evaluated twenty-three public hospitals in the metropolitan region of São Paulo. Only one of them had the minimum quality recommended by PAHO. After this work, I became the manager of the worst hospital in terms of quality, among those who were tested.

This *worst* hospital was the largest public hospital in the East Zone of São Paulo metropolitan region, with 500 beds, poor physical conditions and serious management problems. Management was on the defensive against its two thousand workers and representatives of society about the problems detected in the hospital accreditation process. They were making practical arrangements regarding the priorities for action and the means to be used to improve quality.

Here as management we 'horizontalised', and started dialogues with different stakeholders. This enabled the involvement of all workers in solving the problem, and it actually reduced the time to get it done. Gradually the solidarity between health professionals and users of this public hospital led to good results. We increased from 20 to 80 per cent of the total minimum requirements of hospital quality identified in a year.

One of the most important lessons about the management of this public hospital was realising that list items could act as conversation starters for discussion on quality improvement in health care organisations. Indicators can be utilised as thematic areas for discussion. This was the method used when UNAIDS, a joint United Nations Program on HIV/AIDS, did a review of the deployment of triple antiretroviral therapy in Brazil in 1997. Arguing is not only the best way to make the diagnosis, but also the best way to find solutions and make arrangements for its implementation.

This rich learning process of evaluating organisations contributed to a better understanding of instrumental rationality on the one hand and the practice and the importance of reconstructing complexity through dialogue on the other hand. The understanding that discursively reconstructs organisations differs from the simple choice of effective ways to do things. The discursive reconstruction implies inclusion of the perspective of the agents, and the definition of practical arrangements around the best argument within organisations.

Final thoughts

The question on how to organise work seems particularly relevant when the traditional means of social regulation, money and power, cannot be equated to a more socially just life and to human dignity. The theory of communicative action and discourse of Habermas (1987, 1990) can be valuable in this context.

Habermas (1985) in *Technique and science as ideology* discusses how the young Hegel speaks of the ontology of being, to discuss the relevance of the relationship between work and interaction. Hegel remarked that the constitution of the human being passes through three intertwining dialectics: the use of language, the relationship with others in family and community life, and the use of instruments to work in social production. Our humanity is related to these dynamics. He proposes a formation of the human being from interactions mediated by language that results in redemption of the human dimension of existence, inside and outside of organisations, within this same dynamic. So humanisation of organisations from this perspective happens by introducing more discussion when this is lacking. This implies increased complexity in relation to the environment. This increased complexity forms the space that produces and reproduces the humanity of those who work, expressed in their speech, their arguments and their practical arrangements.

One of the issues that may be specified as an objection to this understanding of discourse theory is whether this kind of communicative action can be performed within each system. Firstly, it should be said that systems are part of the living world and not merely abstract notions. Secondly, Habermas (1990) differentiates the strength of communicative acts depending on contexts. One can say that speech has limitations within organisations, but these limitations should be overcome in order to do justice to all the people involved.

What the description of health care in relation to AIDS in Brazil demonstrates is an opportunity, but it does not intend to submit a list of operational procedures for communicative action within health care organisations in general. A list like this may not be very useful, because in discourse the other can always say no. This makes organising humanisation something for which a blueprint cannot be given – it has to be renegotiated again and again. However, it may help to know what procedures contribute to more interaction, cooperation and discourse within organisations, and what procedures generally hinder these. This distinction allows us to evaluate the relationship between administration procedures and their contribution to maintaining or increasing the organisation's complexity.

If an administrator is for example interested in promoting technological innovation within organisations, one must first of all understand that structured information flows contribute to the execution of repetitive cycles of production and imply reduced complexity. So when you want to innovate, this already structured information will not help. It is necessary to increase the possibilities of interaction mediated by language, including this special mode that is discourse. And work that increases these possibilities of interaction is also an ethical option (Carvalho and Lima, 2009; Lima et al., 2010).

References

Carvalho, L. & Lima, C.R. Montenegro de (2009) 'Informação, comunicação e inovação: gestão da informação para inovação em uma organisação complexa', *Informação & Informação* 14, p. 1–20.
Donabedian, A. (1980) *Explorations in quality assessment and monitoring. Vol. 1: The definitions of quality and approaches to its assessment.* Ann Arbor, MI: Health Administration Press.
Foucault, M. (1973) *The Birth of a Clinic: An Archeology of Medical Perception.* London: Sheridan.
– (1977) 'Verité et pouvoir', *L'Arc* 70, p. 16–26.
Habermas, J. (1990) *Moral consciousness and communicative action.* Cambridge, MA: MIT Press.
– (1985) *Technique and science as ideology.* Boston, MA: Beacon Press.
– (1987) *The Theory of Communicative Action. Vol. 2: Lifeworld and system: A critique of functionalist reason.* Boston, MA: Beacon Press.
Lima, C.R. Montenegro de (2007) *Conselhos de saúde - informação, poder e política social.* Rio de Janeiro: Eaesp.
– (2005) *AIDS - uma epidemia de informações* (2nd ed.) Rio de Janeiro: Liinc.
Lima, C.R. Montenegro de, Tenório, J.R. & Kempner, F. (2010) 'Problematização e racionalização discursiva dos processos produtivos em organisações', *Revista de gestão da tecnologia e sistemas de informação* 7, p. 669–92.
Luhmann, N. (1984) *Introducción a la teoría de sistemas* [Soziale Systeme: Grundriß einer allgemeinen Theorie]. (Trans. J. Torres Nafarrete). Guadalajara; Barcelona: Anthropos.

9 Humanisation of the economy[1]

Christian Felber and Fernando Suárez-Müller

Introduction

The humanisation of society is characterised by the institutional realisation of the principles of human dialogue.[2] Humans are dialogical beings and so the realisation of the principles of dialogue is what we propose to call the process of humanisation. In this 'idealism of dialogue' people cooperate on the basis of ethical values such as symmetry, equality, liberty, openness, renouncement of violence, tolerance, respect, solidarity and responsibility. In light of these values, cooperating for the benefit of *the common good* guides our investigation of the humanisation of the economy. These values constitute an *a priori* of righteousness which is taken for granted each time we engage in dialogue (Apel, 1988). I cannot *really* engage in dialogue without presuming these values to hold, without presupposing that the other person feels a commitment to these same values. To make a free sphere of communication between humans possible, these values need to be acknowledged by the people involved. Today, we are most familiar with these values in the sphere of interpersonal relationships.

The most essential pillar of society responsible for our subsistence – the economy – has come to be seen by many as some kind of natural entity that stands alone and moves and grows following its own rules. Its game is competition. Competition between individuals with individual interests inhibits accounting for that which, in our capitalist society, is thought of as almost old-fashioned and naïve: *the common good*. Although our modern economic system of free competition is not formally built on violence and fear as was once slavery and serfdom, competition nonetheless constitutes an organisational model in which the unethical values of violence and fear are very much alive. A system based on the ideals of humanity (the 'idealism of dialogue') cannot be structured by rules of competition, which require winners and losers.

In light of the question of how to organise humanisation, and how to humanise organisations, we contend in this chapter that changing the current organisation principles of the economy is an integral and vital part of the process of humanisation. We take it to be essential for humankind to move towards an economy based on cooperation. It is possible to humanise the economy if we take cooperation instead of competition as its central organising principle. The ethical values of dialogue need to be integrated in all possible layers of the economic system. In an economy that deserves to be called *humane* these ethical values determine the rules of the game.

The humanisation of the economy ultimately implies the realisation of a system of labour based on collaborative principles which envision the *Common Good* of society –this is a mirroring of our inner dialogical predispositions. In such a *cooperative system of labour* resources will be distributed on an ethical basis. Ethics here becomes an integral part of economics, which is to say that economics becomes part of a social enterprise, of a philosophical reflection concerned with the aims of humanity. The sociologist Nico Stehr calls this development the *moralisation of the markets* (Stehr, 2007; Stehr et al., 2009). This means that the economy (both as a science and as a domain of reality) is progressively being reintegrated into the domain of practical philosophy.

But how to conceive of such an integration? Georg Wilhelm Friedrich Hegel once emphasised that our bourgeois society (capitalism) was based on a model of egoistic subjects that dominated the philosophy of Enlightenment. He emphasised the need to transform this type of society into a system of cooperativeness. Inspired by these thoughts, Karl Marx proposed an economic philosophy that went far beyond Hegel's intentions and conceived a type of labour society that would eradicate all private property. We are now discovering the possibility of an economic system that transcends both capitalism and communism. A theory of humanisation could clarify the philosophical framework for such a system. Critically, in the dialogical theory of humanisation proposed here, freedom and responsibility, and respect for individuality and solidarity, go hand in hand.

To begin our discussion we first investigate a major fallacy in current views on the economy, which takes the market economy necessarily to be based on competition. The values of dialogue can and should be regulative for the economic domain. We will show that this would make our economy more consistent with the values of modernity, which found their expression with the motto of the French Revolution (liberty, equality, fraternity). The values of modernity are in fact a constitutive part of the interdependent values of dialogue. After that discussion, we will expound upon an example of an international organisation of entrepreneurs that takes this mission of humanising the economy seriously.

Oikonomía and the values of modernity[3]

The Greek called the science of the household *oikonomía*. Sharing and responsibility (two principles of dialogue) were the dominant values of the household and in fact this has not changed (Aristotle, 1977, III). Of course there is no need to romanticise the Greek system since we all know that it was based on slavery, women were not equals and patriarchal attitudes would probably have been very common. Nonetheless the theory of *oikonomía*, as was developed by Aristotle, was based on the idea of small communities dedicated to the common good and based on interpersonal values and imperatives of responsibility. In this science of *oikonomía* economic imperatives were always considered within the scope of ethical rules. The economy of a nation (the polis) was perceived as an interrelation, a network of households (*oikoi*). The idea of a well-ordered state, a *politeía* as Plato had already called it, was a major preoccupation of Greek philosophy. In it no part of society escapes the ethical rules.

The central values of modernity, developed during the French Revolution, are freedom, equality and fraternity. These values are taken to be regulative for all practices in modern society. If thought through, it is not hard to see that these values of modernity correspond to central values of dialogue. These principles cannot be traded in one for the other – they presuppose each other and are dialogical amongst themselves. They need to be in balance when realised in practice. We will now briefly discuss these values and show how the modern economy and society do not think through the basic interdependence of these three values.

Liberty

One of the main values determining our modern concept of humanity is certainly liberty. This term is fundamental for all progressive movements, and also for less progressive ones. Even the most tyrannical regimes of the past century, Stalinism and Nazism, claim a legitimation based on the term. Liberty is certainly the highest legitimation value of modern expansionist capitalism. In a certain sense it is the most harmless value of the French Revolution for the modern growth paradigm (Wal, 2004, p. 18). This ideal gives liberalism and neoliberalism their name. Today, in Western industrialised countries, only a fanatic minority would refuse to accept political liberalism understood as democratic tolerance of other opinions. Neoliberalism radicalises economic liberalism and wants us to believe that liberty just offers one choice (and in fact no choice at all – there is no alternative, as Margaret Thatcher once said), which is the maximisation of free trade. To Friedrich von Hayek and Milton Friedman the only resting option is slavery (Hayek, 2007; Friedman, 2002). To them, expansive capitalism is a necessary condition of political freedom. According to them the fundamental rights of humankind are private property and competition that, being basic, should preferably not be limited in any circumstance. In this sense neoliberalism is in fact a hypertrophy of the atomistic model of society defended by empiricist and sceptical philosophers of the Enlightenment.

Within (neo)liberalism, liberty is not thought through, thus becoming independent of other values, especially equality and fraternity. If we take the word in its original meaning we could say that this position 'perverts' liberty (perversio = Latin for turning something against its original sense). Ethical values and economic thought and action have come to be seen as altogether different domains. The economy is seen primarily as a natural entity, with its own natural laws and rules legitimating competition, blind efficiency and the unlimited pursuit of profit. Only in the sphere of interpersonal relationships do we expect humanist values such as solidarity, mutual help and sharing. This false separation that allows the economy to be ruled by different values from those characterising human relationships is the product of the modern science of economics, which takes the liberty of the rational individual as its starting point and takes the market to be something abstract, autonomous, separated from other domains of society. It is the cultural achievement of modern capitalism to integrate this abstraction within a frame of legitimacy and legality. The law now represents capitalism. It has become completely natural to subdue people to market imperatives, to violate the dignity of humankind in the name of this one-sided rationality, and to destroy our environmental and social ties in the name of efficiency and profit. It is taken to be a natural thing that people should become a kind of predator in the global trading business. It is seen as successful to increase capital by cutting jobs, and to let others work for us is taken to be a personal accomplishment.

Equality

Liberty, taken on itself, thus leads to exploitation and isolation. But true liberty cannot stand on itself and needs equality and fraternity. If liberty is not the unlimited expansion of the will, it is the ability of the will to set itself boundaries. In true liberty, the will turns towards an encounter with the *equal*. This seems to culminate in a sentiment of affection for the other that we call love. The equal is not identical, since it is different, but it is symmetrical and, in a sense, part of a higher unity comprising the equals. In various senses equality is the end of liberty since liberty moves towards the equal but the equal limits personal freedom. Humankind is the only species capable of reflecting on these processes and any human will automatically recognise other beings capable of this reflection to be its equals. But this does not automatically imply the recognition of equality. An enemy is recognised as an equal that endangers my dignity and that is therefore rejected, which means that the initial recognition is finally refused.

A pure system of economic competition is based on the idea of existential selection – the existence of the competing other must be annihilated. This cannot be compared with a mere sporting event since the basis of the economy, labour, is the individual effort to secure survival. To create or maintain a system of competition is to create or maintain a system in which there are losers and winners, in which some lose their jobs in order to secure gains for others.[4] This creates and maintains a system of distrust that generates oppositions. In a society of isolated individuals the state becomes a formal and external disciplinary machine that has to secure individual rights without being an object of identification.

Fraternity

Equality can only be achieved to the extent that people have equal opportunities. Potentiating equality of opportunities also gets us to ideas of self-responsibility and autonomy. Equality should never be reduced to uniformity, as this would imply a collectivist model in which individual differences were ignored. Liberty, equality and fraternity are in fact values defining the higher value of justice. Ignoring individual differences would annihilate the idea of a correlation of liberty, equality and fraternity, and make the whole enterprise of humanisation senseless. Only when people have similar opportunities can society become something more than a compound of single unities. There can only be real cooperation if people are equals and consider each other to be equals. Liberty and equality are therefore a precondition for fraternity. Real fraternity comes from the inside. Autonomy is the acknowledgement of the moral law that resides in us and speaks to us. This moral law speaks of justice, of *doing justice to all entities* on earth (not just to humans). Justice is in fact about the dignity of things. But it is a cooperative enterprise to understand this voice coming from inside oneself. This cooperative effort was once ritualised and called *church*.

The economy is an integral part of social life and is itself part of our interpersonal relationships. The values that constitute the centre of society, especially equality and fraternity, that make relationships between parents, children, friends, and neighbours prosper – these values should be carried inside the economic domain and they should determine our economic way of life. The idea that human values of equality and fraternity function only in the small and private domain of familiar and close relationships is a clear underestimation of humankind. These values can and should be put to work at organisations and globally. The economic discourse of ancient philosophy can be rediscovered in order to understand what a 'moralisation of the markets' means; the dialogically connected values of modernity can be a source of inspiration. The laws determining the economy are only fallaciously independent from the cultural and political settings in which they are immersed. A 'Greek approach' is needed that connects all social domains to ethical values, and a modern approach that balances liberty, equality and fraternity.

Economy for the Common Good

The question is, of course, how? What does it mean to take the dialogical values of interpersonal relationships that include the modern threesome as principles to guide management decisions? A crucial part of the theory of humanisation[5] is that the 'recipients' of humanising processes can be non-humans. An organisation can be seen as though it were a human constantly in conversation with entities that are supposed to have rights and that may be humans or not. Of course an organisation cannot actually 'talk' to many partners involved, such as the whole community in which factory workers live, or the environment, which might suffer from certain production methods. However, it is possible to question oneself: What would a dialogical attitude towards such partners imply? What would an attitude of equality, solidarity, true renouncement of violence look like? What would it be when, to the best of my ability, I would try to act in the interest of the common good?

Over the last few decades many practices of corporate social responsibility (CSR) have been developed (Crane et al., 2008). They are a symptom of the 'moralisation of the markets' referred to above. However, although this is a good development, the CSR activities of most organisations are only aiming at an improvement of the ethical dimension of their own enterprises. This is an implementation of the value of non-violence, but on itself this all too often does not amount to more than reducing harm. The basic and most problematic assumption of our economic activities is not questioned – that companies compete to optimise profit without benefiting the common good.

That we might challenge this is exemplified by *Economy of the Common Good*, a network organisation that tries seriously to think through the idea that any individual company or organisation can take the common good as its leading orientation.

According to *Economy for the Common Good* the motto of the French Revolution, 'liberté, égalité, fraternité', should be read following the order of the words: freedom comes first – but only as long as it makes equality and fraternity possible. Cooperation rather than competition should define the content of liberty. Real liberty is about the necessity of limiting itself when meeting others (Felber, 2009). Liberty should not be understood as a form of unlimited expansionism, but as the desire to encounter a boundary outside us that induces us to cooperate. Free development cannot be understood in a merely expansive way; it is first of all a process of Bildung, of formation and constitution of the self. To guarantee a supportive income for all and to realise the idea of Bildung as a basis for moral reflection that helps to develop a broad sense of responsibility are both fundamental issues related to the idea of personal freedom and political liberty as conceived in the context of an economy for the common good. Labour organisations, in which people spend most time of their life in order to make a living, should also attend this need of Bildung.[6]

This has nothing to do with continuous growth. Freedom brings us to cooperation, which is a strategy of survival. Humanity's survival has been determined by its capacity to cooperate. To relate liberty with continuous growth is probably connected with the modern idea that there is nothing beyond life; the ultimate goal of life seems to be just to survive and to do this as comfortably as possible. The natural tendency of humans to seek self-affirmation through communication with others ends up in the need to get recognised by others through the admiration resulting from an unlimited accumulation of money[7] – money being the expression of the possibility to have and to do what we want. Happiness is then wrongly measured as the expansion of the will, whereas the will is in fact, as we see it, seeking to set down moral boundaries within which it can develop itself in cooperation with others. To *Economy for the Common Good* the exemplary model that serves as a guideline for all types of labour organisations is the cooperative. This model is neither collectivistic nor individualistic, but a synthesis of both.

What makes the member-organisations of *Economy for the Common Good* different is that they develop a vision about how the whole of society should be structured.

The organisations within *Economy for the Common Good* actually try to think through what their position is and should be with regard to the global economies and societies. They are creating a network of ethical entrepreneurship with the aim of changing the whole of society, and consequently the whole of the economy, in a well-determined direction. Real political liberalism requires broad political participation. *Economy for the Common Good* proposes the combination of political and economic participation: democratic processes should not only be broadened in society, they should also be installed in the meso-level of organisations and companies. *Economy for the Common Good* therefore not only sets out to elaborate a CSR document that is freely available for all companies which want to adhere to the network, it also sets out to begin transforming the overall structure of the global economy. Therefore it is also a platform for ideas about how to change the political system, how to elaborate and implement new forms of democracy, and, even more importantly, about how to help change each other's infrastructural mentality and attitudes, which have been seriously affected by the long cultural period of modern capitalistic expansionism (Welzer, 2013, p. 64). Its activities are therefore not only concerned with corporations, but with all kinds of social organisations (they are strictly speaking not just a CSR strategy but also an OSR strategy, a strategy for social responsibility in all kinds of *Organisations*). Many of these ideas have been taken up in the book that gave this organisation its name (Felber, 2010).

Democratisation

Economy for the Common Good strives to promote forms of community life. People can get mobilised around initiatives working with memberships in which, on different levels of society, processes of democratisation can create a system of cascading democracy that unites representative, direct and participative forms of democracy. Engagement is what makes these memberships possible. Society is not conceived as a sum of individuals united by an abstract state, but as a circle of circles, as it is called in the Platonic tradition, each circle being a community that can include many communities or be in touch with other communities on different levels.

Economic convent

Another idea developed by *Economy for the Common Good* is the creation of an economic convent ('con-venire', coming together) in order to define (for a determinate time) what the common good is. Different stakeholders would participate in the formulation of a document of ethical and ecological standards, which would then be voted on by all citizens. The rationale of such a convent is the idea that the ultimate value of corporations is not to make profit by way of competition. The ultimate goal is not profit in itself, but the development of an ethical and social attitude using as much money as possible to strengthen the common good and consequently cooperation. Organisations should be able to expect support for this kind of attitude. This support should not just be left up to consumer citizenship; instead, a whole organisational network should be involved in a web of assistance. Organisations committed to the common good should support each other and support those companies that take their ethical standards seriously. Municipalities and local authorities can support enterprises committed to the common good by giving them priority in open tenders, or by reducing their taxes. Governments can approve laws to encourage organisations to have ethical attitudes.

Financial profits

These should thus be seen as means and not ends. Profits should be reinvested in society. Profits can be used for investment in labour and innovation but only if certain social and ethical standards are met. Profits should not go to people who do not work in the company unless there are social or ethical reasons. This of course has repercussions for shareholding in general, since capital shares directly benefit the individual pockets and not the common good. Neither should profits be used to support political parties. The general idea is that in organisations there should always be an ethical discussion about where the profits flow.

Establishing a democratic bank

This would not be a profit-oriented bank and would strictly limit its investments to supporting enterprises adhering to the common good network. Credit would be based on savings and there are no accountancy tricks to create new money. There are neither lending nor savings rates, just a fee to cover costs and inflation. The democratic bank shows savers what happens to their money and makes it possible for them to determine where it goes. When banks and enterprises are freed from dealing with interest they will also be freed from compulsory growth.

The commons

Essential infrastructures of our economy should remain under the control of citizens and should neither belong to private companies nor to the state. This has nothing to do with communism or Marxism; the discussion on the commons goes back to the times of Plato and Aristotle (Radkau, 2008; Ostrom, 1990). The idea is not to abolish property itself, but to abolish 'expansionist property'. As Thomas Piketty has shown, the increasing inequality in our societies is contrary to the basic principles of a democratic social state in which there should exist equal rights and equal access to participation (Piketty, 2013, p. 671–84 and p. 751–92). That the unlimited accumulation of property endangers the planet hardly needs saying (Daly, 1994, 1991; Paech, 2011). The *positive tendency* to inequality must be reversed by a *negative tendency* that restores equilibrium. The idea is to control economic expansionism. At the micro-level, inequality among individuals can be influenced (creating a negative feedback) with laws limiting wage development and property. At the meso-level inequality among organisations can be influenced (creating a negative feedback) by controlling the size and property of enterprises. At the macro-level our whole society should develop a negative feedback by setting limits to economic and human expansionism. The idea of setting negative feedback limits to property was proposed by Plato (although of course he did not use the language of systems theory) and was rediscovered later within British Idealism, and then it served as a model for William Beveridge's concept of the modern social state (functioning by means of taxes) in which it mainly functioned to improve social infrastructures and financial redistributions (Beveridge, 1942).

Concluding remarks

The idea of the common good cannot just be identified with a project of universal solidarity. This is only an aspect of what fraternity really means. In a sense 'solidarity' is just a correctional social measure to overcome the isolation of citizens. When solidarity comes from the inside we are approaching fraternity, but this type of solidarity is not just an emotion: it is the openness of the mind to the inner call demanding us to labour for a community of the soul with all living creatures. The economic system is not something separated from this moral domain; it is in fact its major road of completeness in a way that is very different from the individual promises of puritan Calvinism, which laid the basis of modern liberalism (Weber, 2012, p. 80–147). The idea of an economy for the common good continues the project of modernity by rationalising the dialogical connection of 'liberty, equality, fraternity' to its ultimate end, but at the same time it transcends modernity by identifying secularism as a representation of early modern atomistic isolationism. The international organisation of entrepreneurs *Economy for the Common Good* is not a utopia but an example of how current enterprises can find their own way in humanising the economy. These entrepreneurs do not just focus on their own companies and have set up a number of initiatives and goals (democratisation, convents, benefits, financial structures, reinforcing the commons) that may be inspiring for all those who feel the need to change their organisations in order to make a contribution to the humanisation of the economy. The *Economy for the Common Good* project is constantly changing; the network created is like a living organism that adapts to all possible new insights and challenges. All their efforts however are focused on the realisation of a cooperative system of labour. To the Greeks, the market (agora) was not just a place of commerce; it was also the instantiation of the 'idealism of dialogue'.

Notes

1 This text links the theory of humanisation proposed by Fernando Suárez-Müller in this volume with the ideas of Christian Felber. Parts of the text can be found in Christian Felber (2008, p. 266–327). Suárez-Müller is responsible for translations of passages from the work of Felber.
2 See '*The process of humanisation*', Chapter 1 in this volume.
3 We dedicate this section to Yanis Varoufakis (see Varoufakis, 2013).
4 Ulrich Beck reserves the term 'Angstgesellschaft' ('society of anxiety') for our current risk society, but the term can be employed to characterise modern competitive capitalism in general (Beck, 2007, p. 28).
5 See, Chapter 1 on humanisation by F. Suárez-Müller's earlier in this volume.
6 For the importance of the notion of Bildung, see Chapter 5 by Schreurs.
7 It was Adam Smith who related capitalism with the desire of man to get recognition from others. See 'Of the nature of self-deceit' (Smith, 2009, p. 180–86).

References

Apel, K.O. (1988) *Diskurs und Verantwortung*. Frankfurt am Main: Suhrkamp.
Aristotle (1977) *Oeconomica*. London: Loeb.
Beck, U. (2007) *Weltrisikogesellschaft*. Frankfurt am Main: Suhrkamp.
Beveridge, W. (1942) *Social insurance and allied services* (online). www.ncbi.nlm.nih.gov/pmc/articles/PMC2560775/pdf/10916922.pdf (accessed on 18-4-2016).
Crane, A., Matten, D., McWilliams, A., Moon, J. & Siegel, D.S. (2008) *The Oxford handbook of corporate social responsibility*. Oxford: Oxford University Press.
Daly, H. (1994) *For the common good*. Boston: Beacon.
– (1991) *Steady-state economics*. Washington: Island Press.
Felber, C. (2008) *Neue Werte für die Wirtschaft*. Vienna: Deuticke.
– (2009) *Kooperation statt Konkurrenz*. Vienna: Deuticke.
– (2010) *Die Gemeinwohl-Ökonomie. Das Wirtschaftsmodell der Zukunft*. Vienna: Deuticke.
Friedman, M. (2002) *Capitalism and freedom*. Chicago: Univ. Chicago Press.
Hayek, F. von (2007) *The road to serfdom*. Chicago: Univ. Chicago Press.

Ostrom, E. (1990) *Governing the commons: The evolution of institutions for collective action.* Cambridge/New York: Cambridge Univ. Press.
Paech, N. (2011) *Befreiung vom Überfluss. Auf dem Weg in die Postwachstumsökonomie.* München: Oekom.
Piketty, T. (2013) *Le capital au XXIe siècle.* Paris: Seuil.
Radkau, J. (2008) *Nature and power: A global history of the environment.* Cambridge/New York: Cambridge Univ. Press.
Stehr, N. (2007) *Die Moralisierung der Märkte.* Frankfurt am Main: Suhrkamp.
Stehr, N., Henning, C. & Weiler, B. (eds) (2009) *The moralization of the markets.* New Brunswick/London: Transaction.
Smith, A. (2009) *The theory of moral sentiments.* London/New York: Penguin.
Smith, A. (2010) *The theory of moral sentiment.* New York: Dover.
Varoufakis, Y. (2013) *A modest proposal for resolving the Eurozone crisis* (online). https://yanisvaroufakis.eu/euro-crisis/modest-proposal/ https://varoufakis.files.wordpress.com/2013/07/a-modest-proposal-for-resolving-the-eurozone-crisis-version-4-0-final1.pdf (accessed on 18-4-2016).
Wal, K. van der (ed.) (2004) *Vrijheid, Gelijkheid en Broederschap?* Budel: Damon.
Weber, M. (2012) *Die protestantische Ethik und der Geist des Kapitalismus.* Darmstadt: Wbg.
Welzer, H. (2013) *Selbst Denken. Eine Anleitung zum Widerstand.* Frankfurt am Main: Fischer.

Index

accountability: for the common good opposed to competition 79; of democratic bank 85; education and managerial discourse of public 42; learning does not fit 46; management effort towards 13; in modernity 63; of the self xv; public xviii; sense does not fit 17; opposed to responsibility 45, 47; and space for uncertainty 48; of students 43; unaccountable experience xvii
actor: in dialogue 4; of humanisation 1–2; prison as theatre, management as 56; of rational reconstruction 74
administration: administrative rules end discussion xxiv; Clinton xiii; skills, techniques and imagination used for xxvi; educators work becomes 35, 37; health care xxvii; maintaining organisational complexity 78; quality quantified in administrative discourse 42; self direction versus vertical 50–3; teaching health 75; in theory of communicative action 71–2
Adorno, T. xiv, xv, xvii, 6
advertising xxv, 62–70: characteristics of industry 61–3; exemplary for managing liquidity 69–70; based on human relationship 65; industry relies on engagement xxvii; liquidity and technology, synopticon 64–5; and liquid modernity 64; public, private, online employee life in ad agency 66–9
advice: advisor training xxii; to board of psychiatric clinic 54; by consultants 20; critique of management 17; humanistic advisory work 30
affectivity: influence on thought 3; in familial discourse 8; and rationality not opposed 6; sentiment of equals 81
alienation: through asymetrical power xxvi; in closed societies 7; and Enlightenment 6; personal experience in psychiatric clinic 58; as possibility in normative anthropology 3; from sense through language 15; and technology 30–1; of work in vertical power structure 52–3, 59
Alon, S. 45
ambiguity: in education 47; organisations need 12–13

analysis: as distance of thinking to object 14; and intuition 15; of modernity (Bauman) 63; practice before 12; opposed to practice 12; precedence over everyday life 24; reconstructing complexity through discourse 76; and scientific management 20–22
anthropology: of organisation xxvi–ii; by Suárez-Müller xxiv; by Stiegler xxv; need for philosophical 3; based on dialogue 3–4; shows will to truth 7; humanist 30; relating human to technics 31; anthropomorphic xii anthropocentric 38
Apel, K.-O. 4, 79
Archimedes, uncertainty versus point of Archimedes in education 48
Arendt, H.: and evil in managing prison 57; and natality in education 48
articulation: articulate citizen 6; capitalism incorporates unarticulated interests xviii; of desirable world 3, 5; of dignity in dialogue xxiv; of moral insights as *differentia specifica* 3; and sense 14, 16–18; *see also language; speech*
Aristotle: and common good 80, 85; economic/household theory 80; human-animal distinction xv; and virtue of balance 50
assembly line: in *liquid modernity* 63; passing doors in psychiatric clinic as 58; versus self directed action, individuality, common good 53; and scientific management 21, 23
authenticity xxiii; versus calculability in education 47; in dialogue 6; in online interaction 69–70; and technology 31
autonomy: as acknowledgement of moral law 82; anarchist 56; capitalism and loss of xviii; of (capitalist) economy 81; of definition of the 'inhuman' xvii; dignity constituted by relational 50; and ethics in anthropological theory of technology 31, 33–5; in humanist education 43; organological conditions of 38; of sense making 7; of subsystems 8; standardisation pressures professional 49; professional 52; public organisations restrain 58; question restriction of 59; *takes time* 37; technics as medicine enabling xxv–vi

Banerjee, S.B. xiii
Barthes, R. 15
Barry, D. 12
Bataille, G. xvii
Baudrillard, J. 13
Bauer, 4
Bauman, Z. xxvii, 61, 63–6, 69–70
Beer, 22
Bergson, H. 15, 24, 27
being: *becoming community* 5; becoming versus 34, contains human rights in essence 5; dialogical structure of 4; happiness as feeling harmony with 7; imagining transcendent 3
Bentham, J. 64
Biesta, G. 30, 38, 46, 48
Beveridge, W. 85
Bildung: and civilisation 6; as different from goals of goal of OECD/PISA 36; and paideia xxvi; and system of knowledge 8; uncertainty as key to 41; uncertainty and responsibility versus intstrumentality, accountability 45–8
biology: biological, cultural and philosophical anthropology 3; economic equals biopolitical status xiii; evolution of *homo sapiens* 3–4; human capable of exceeding programmatic 32; intergenerational learning based in 38n4; related to subsystems of society 8
Bishop, M. xviii
Blanchot, M. 5
Böhler, D. 4
Bonger, 51
Botter, J. 52
Brandom, R. 5
Bregman, R. 46
Bricmont, J. 12
Brink, G. 52–3
Buffet, W. xviii
bureaucracy: authentic interaction not 70; non-bureaucratic management of ad industry 69; bureaucratic rationalisation (through scientific models) of life in medical practice 72–3; bureaucratisation versus *liquid* ad industry xxvii; education transformed into bureaucratic culture 46; humanising rationalisation turns into dehumanising bureaucratisation 50–3; 'inhuman' xvii; as organisation of modernity 63; liquidity of ad industry opposed to 64
Burrel, G. xi, 23
Bush, G.W. xii
Butler, J. xiv, xv, xvii

capitalism 30: not accounting for common good 79; and competition xxviii, 79; CSR strategies to transform expansionist 84; Hegel on 80; including/excluding/defining human/inhuman xii, xvii; liberty as legitimation of 81; as 'society of anxiety' 86n4; transcending communism and 80

capability (*also capacity*): to abstract from everyday time 24; of community to define human xiv; of cooperation 83; creative xv; essential, dialogical xxii, xxiv, 3–4, 6; for ethics inhibited by new tools 37; humanisation initiated by experience, position and intellectual 51; of imagination and desire 33; incapacity by every new 34; intellectual versus intelligence 47; public institutions engagement with all stakeholders' 59; of public institutions for systematic humiliation 56–7; reflection as exclusively human 82; of self-direction versus machine 53; for self-direction relationally embedded 50; of self-direction and vertical, public organisation 52; as skill (*see skill*) 32
care: anxious neoliberalism and xviii; applying humanisation to xxiii; autonomy, technology and 33–4; *cinematograpic tendency* opposed to 24; conversation to make organisations 18; extending care for society and planet 8, 9; of holding company versus management 64; humanism and 35; of ICT in education 70–1; mission statements and loss of 13; in Renaissance prison reform 51; and solidarity promotes happiness 7; to not stabilise interaction 70; thinking about or from 14, 18; *see also health care*
Carlos, J. xi–xii
Carvalho, L. 76, 78
change [concept]: in ad industry in liquid modernity 61–70; business not committed to social xviii; in civilisation 6; common sense agreement to 11; of contexts and technics make humanisation never ending 34–5; of health care in dealing with AIDS epidemic 72–8; heteronomy by ICT's constant 37; historical institutional 1–2; humanising as moral/political sensibility to 18; *human value as guide to* 54; inherent moral imperative to 9; language's possibility for xvi; learning to deal with xxvi, 48; personal experience leading to 58; and repetition of organisation and knowledge 23–4; and striving for immortality xi
Charlie Chaplin 53
Chia, R. 22
Churchman, C.W. 22
citizen: alienated from public institutions 53; articulate 6; and Bildung 46; as consumer 84; as controller economy 85; decent society does not humiliate 56; is not isolated individual 85; of liberal democracy manipulated xvii; in *Modernity and the Holocaust* 63; rights on identity of xiii; as *terminus ad quem* of humanisation 2
civilisation: dealing with punishment as test of 56; defining who's in need of xxi; dehumanisation born of Western modernity's 63; and humanisation 5–6

Coeckelbergh, M. on alienation by technology 30–1; on skill 34
common: consultants have in 20; sense 14, 25–26; *Economy for common good* 82–6; experience and search for meaning 17; Good xxii, xxviii, 8, 53, 75, 80–6; mission statement 13; moral and religious values constitutive of US xii; understanding of justice xv; world xvi
community: *becoming*, 5; and capitalism xviii; by conversation as search for morality, ethos and sense 17 (*see also* 24 'joint venture'); democratisation 84; founding of xii, xiv; health care 74–5; Hegel on 77–8; including all speeches in 76; with all life 86; moral 5, 7; individualisation opposed to 39n8; organisation related to 83; responsible versus accountable 45
communication xxi, xxvi, xxviii, 18, 30: in ad industry 61–2, 67, 69; discursiveness and presentativeness 16; Enlightenment and space of free, rational 6; expanding community of 76; and formation of subjectivity 71–2; Goffman for restructuring 56; Habermas and xvi, xxvii, 4; in liberal economy 83; in meetings 18; Merleau-Ponty, Apel, Böhler on 4; open society and free 5; presupposed values 79; Ranciere on xvi; of rationalities, Foucault 73
competition xviii: versus cooperation xxviii, 8–9, 79–84; and meritocracy 45
complexity xxv, xxvii: reducing xxviii, 36, 72–3, 76; expert knowledge harmful to 20–25; and uncertainty 47; reconstructing 74, 76–8
consultancy xxv, 20–27: to psychiatric clinic 54
consumer xxvii: mass xvii; ad industry humanising relation to 64–70; citizenship 84
control xi, xxvi, 64, 68, 76: biopolitical 72–3; economic 8; of economy by citizen 85; humanising rationalisation of 50; of 'inhuman' xvii; of life by oneself 1, 7; and loss of meaning 18; management, education and 35–6, 41–9; and modernity 63; in prison 54–55, 58; in public organisation 52–3, 57; of reality and experience 11–13
Coornhert, D.V. 51
cooperation xxviii: based in dialogue 4; economy based on 9, 79, 83–4; and equality 82; in health organisation 78; OECD 36
Corcoran, S. xvii–iii
Gragg, W. xii, xviii
Crane, A. 83
creativity xxi: of ad agency employees 27, 62, 64; Bildung and 41; 'creative capitalism' xviii; educating intellectuality and 47; as intrinsic motivation 49; of knowledge and problematisation 22–27; of language and subjectification xiv–xvi; of organisations 23; of repetition and change 23; students need uncertainty for 44, 48
CSR 83, 84

culture: macro-level humanisation 2; versus civilisation 6; as transindividuation (with technics) 33, 38; poisoned 35; of care in education 37; democratic into bureaucratic educational 46; of accounting 48; of control in clinic 55; of fostering relationships in advertising 65
curiosity: of consultant 25; in education 43, 48
Cusanus, N. 13, 14
Czerniawska, F. 20

Daly, H. 85
Damasion, A. 3
dehumanisation xxvi, xxvii, 2, 11: during AIDS epidemic 73; agreement about xxi; alienation as 30, 31; when culture becomes poisoned 35; effect of corporations on ad agencies 62; by expert consultancy 25; in humanism 31; through isolation from communication 71; and modernity 63; and relational autonomy 50; rationalisation of public institutions become 52; by technology 30, 35
Deleuze, G. 23
Delistrati, C.C. 66
democratisation: in all aspects of society 84; of education into bureaucracy 46; as expression of dialogue in structure of society and state 5–9; as goal of entrepreneurs 86; of health care 75; inequality counters 85; political liberalism and xvii, 81
Deotte, J.L. xvi–xvii
Derrida, J. 13
Derkx, P. 34, 35
desire: of ad agency employees 61, 64, 67; based in technics 32–5; for better world 3, 16; for certainty/security 46–7; for cooperation 83; development as intrinsic 4; for domination 63; for efficiency, transparency 37; family as expression of 8; of health care leaders 75; for meaning 14; for sense-making 14
development xxii, xxiii: of autonomy in public institution 50, 52; community xviii, 75; of ethos 18; of health administrator 71; of humanity xv, xxiv, 1–9, 34, 50; of human relations in advertising 69; of institutions xxv, xxvi; liberty is not expansionist 83; of *moralisation of the markets* 80–85; organisational xxi, xxvii; of questions as goal of organisation theory 23; of students 41–2; of systems of punishment 51; technical, social and human co-constituted 31–8
Dewey, J. 3
dialogical: approach to problems 20–21; approach to education 47, 48; attitude xxiv, 9, 83; capacity/capability xxii, xxiv, 4, 6; consultancy methods 21; mind 5; nature (human) 6, 79; organisations 30, 83; power 4, 5; practice xxiv; principles 7, 9, 79; process 5,

6, 7, 21, 47; relation of individual, social and technical 32; reason 8; structure 6; values xxii, xxiv, 80, 82, 86

dialogue: xxii–iv, xxvii–viii, in education 36, 44–5, 47–8, 52; *idealism of* 4–6, 86 (*see also* 30); as meaningful opposed to expert, external knowledge and solutions 20–21, 23, 26–27; in organising health care 74, 76–7; about technics 32, 37–8; and types of organisations 8; values of 79–80; as value in Western thinking 35; and vertical power (of public institutions) 52–5, 57, 59

dignity 3, 22: capitalist violation of 81; constituted by dialogue xxii, xxiv, 4–5; and discourse in health care 73, 77; and fraternity 82; and humanism xxiii, 34–5, 51; and public institutions xxvi, 50–3, 56; relational autonomy and 53

discipline: in competitive economy 82; and freedom balanced in public institution 50, 53, 57, 59; of HIV/AIDS patient 72; *panopticon/synopticon* 64; in prison 51–2, 4; of students 42–6

discourse 8, 18: ancient economic 82; and communicative action 74; creative xv; of dignity of HIV/AIDS victims 73; about education management 42–6 (also 30); execution of power through xvii, xxvii, 53; of health professionals 75, 77; human rights xi; reconstructing complexity through 76, 78; and 'rest' xvi, 16; about technology 30–4

discursive: and existential and ethical problems 22; implicit norms 5; reality 16–18; reconstruction of diversity 77

discussion: excluded from/silenced in xxi, xxiv, xxv, xxvii 12–13, 16, 23, 36, 45; as mode of meeting 17; need for 11, 21, 24, 37, 59, 72, 75–8, 85; original meaning of *consultare* 20, 22, 25–7; and 'rest' 16

diversity xxii–iii; confronting students with 41, 48; consultancy logic reducing 20–23, 25; and imagination 38; managerial ideals opposed to 12; of perspectives in common sense 25–27

Dobson, J. xvii

Donabedian, A. 77

Dr. van Mesdag clinic 54, 57

ecology: from ego- to eco-directed organisation 52; humanisation of 1, 2, 5; and logics of progress 7; in economic convent 84; non-anthropocentric 9n3 (cf 38n2); *see also nature*

economy: xxiv; of cooperation xxviii, 79–80; depends on ICT 30; for the Common Good 82–6; relevance of public health for 75; as subsystem of society 8–9; and values of modernity 80–2

Edwards, M. xviii

Elias, N. 6

Elmers, M. 12

education: and control xxvii, 30, 35, 37, 41–9, 52; culture of care in 37; ICT in 30–37; 'hidden curriculum' 44; horizontal versus vertical in public 52, humanist xxii–iii; 56–7; and imagination 36, 38; and meritocracy 45–7; *paideia* xxv; in prison 51, 58; responsibility versus accountability in 47–9, and public health care 75; and uncertainty 41–9; *see also Bildung*

efficiency: of accounting 48; economic 8, 64, 81; and ICT xxvi, 36–8; inefficient bodies xiii; as organisational goal xxi, 53; of philantrocapitalism xviii; as pillar of quality in care 77; and scientific management 21, 27; opposed to weak thinking 18; *see also control*

emotion: and basic trust 41; in communication 6; deep emotionality 3; fraternity is more than 86; in *romantisation* next to Enlightenment 6

empowerment: and Enlightenment 6; in education 45; in public organisation 52–3; and social media 70; *see also alienation*

Enlightenment/enlightenment: as liberation of dialogue 6; egoistic subject of philosophy of 80–1

Epimetheus 32

equality: and common good 85; as dialogical value xxii–iii, 4, 9, 79–80–3, 85; health in inequal society 71; of human/non-human xi–xii; and individuation 35; political xiv–xvi; *Public* organisation and formal inequality 52, 58–9

Erikson, E. 41

essence: of Black Lives Matter xii; of human in: moral reasoning 3, thinking 3, imagination 3; emotionality 3, use of tools 3, dialogue xxiv–v, 4, 30, language xvi, reflection xxvi, will to truth 7; of humanism 34; humanity has no xxv, 34–5; life is ambiguous, uncertain in 47; of meeting versus conversation 17; of meritocracy xxvi, 45; of needed economic change 79, 85; philosophical anthropology of human 3–6; of problem of education 38; of public organisations 53; *relationship* human, technical, social not 32; 'Seinsvergessenheit' of 42; of social media 69; of technology 31–2

esthetic: conversations as 17; formation 8–9; perspective xxiv; politics as xv–xviii

ethics xxi, xxiii, xxviii: ambiguous xiv; and autonomy through (technical) skill 31, 33–4, 37–8; capitalism and xii; of communicative interaction 71–2, 78; economy and 79–85; and efficiency discourse 53; ethos 16–18; and existential problems 22; Goffman and 56; of information ownership 72; and intellectual sympathy 25; and politics, human-animal distinction xv; and reconstruction of complexity 74; of self 2; *universal* 1

Ewijk, H. van 37
exclusion: by defining human/inhuman xii, xiv; information as tool for 73; of patients xxvii, 73, 75; as punishment 50–1; of uncertainty xxvi, 47
existential: ambivalence to ethics xii; desire for security 46; fears of managers 48; problems 22; selection through competition 82; uncertainty 42, 47
experience: ad industry anticipates 61; of consultant 20–3, 25–7; as consumer product 65; and control 11, 42, 53; and imagination and autonomy 32–4; of inhuman xvii, 54, 63; inner 3, 7; of meaning xxii, 17; of patient 74; speech reconfiguring field of xv–xvi; using personal xxiii–vii, 24, 51, 57–9, 76
expert 63; development *takes time* 37; logic of consultancy 20–27; online presence of 68
explicit conversation and making 17–18; dialogical structure in life xxii, 4; educational goals 46; *making it explicit* 5; opposed to sense, ethos, thinking xxii, 13–18; *see also articulation*

feeling: alienation 30, 36, 53; of consultant 26; as consumer product 65; committed to values 79; free to speak online 70; of happiness 7; humiliation 56; of implicit values 12, 14–15; need for change 86; powerless as doctor 71; and rationality xv–xvi, 3–4; responsible 43–4; *see also emotion*
Flusser, V. 37
Forst, R. 4
Foucault, M. xiv, xv, xvii, xxvii, 1–2, 54, 57, 64, 72–73
freedom xxiii, xxiv, xxv; of ad agencies pressured by budgets 62; and discipline in public organisation 50, 52–3; 58–9; of sexual orientation in AIDS discussion 72; through technological skill 32, 35; as value in dialogical theory 80–3
Frey, B. S. 45
Friedman, M. 81
Frissen, V. 30
Fuglsang, M. 23

Gadamer, H. G. 2
Gates, B. xviii
Gewirtz, 46
Giddens, A. 41
Gilroy, P. xiii
globalisation 31; of capitalist power xviii; of democratic power 7; of dialogical values in economy 82, 84; and identity concerns xii
Goffman, I. xxvii, 56
Green, M. xviii

Habermas, J. xxiv, xxvii, xxviii; different from esthetic politics xvi; and emotion 6; and epistemology and practice of reconstructing complexity 74, 76; and intersubjectivity 71, 77–8; and lifeworld (in prison) 57; and rights 4
happiness: maximising 7; and money 83; and open society 5
Hardt, M. xvii
Hayek, F. 81
health care: xxv, and child's trust 41; and discourse, communicative action 71–8; excluding patients xxvii, 73–4; medicine, bureaucracy and 72–4; negotiating vertical-horizontal tension 56–7; policies in public sphere (Brazil) 74–6; quality 76–7; reconstructing complexity in 74
Hegel, G.W.F. xxiv; on capitalism and cooperation 80; and Enlightenment 6; 77; and intersubjectivity 77–8
Heidegger, M.: and forgetting existential questions 42; on thinking 14
hermeneutic: circle and self 2, 4; of confidence (in language) xvi; humanism and xxiii; of relation between individual, social and technological 38
hierarchy: education, meritocracy and 45; *liquid modernity* and 63; moral xiv; in public organisation 52
history: colonial xxi; of Dutch prison system 50–1, 56, 58; humanist Renaissance interest in xxiii; end of 9; humanisation in light of xxiv, 1; individual subsumed to xiii; progress in biological and cultural 3, 7; technological basis of 33–5
HIV/AIDS xxiii, xxvii; 71–8
Hofstadter, R. 47
Hoogervorst, J. R. H. 51
Horkheimer, M. 6
Hösle, V. 8
Höpfl, H. J. 19
Houten, D. van 1, 9
Huijer, M. 50
humanism: humanisation and Dutch xxii–xxiii, 34; Chapters in context of xxiv; new dialogical 6; relation to technology 37; mixing normative and descriptive humanity 50
humanist: anthropology 30; anti xxi, 30, 57; balance of freedom and self-direction 50; dialogue as essential to 32; ideal opposed to technics as human 34; prison reform 51; university xxii, 43; trans 30–1; tradition of Bildung 48; values not separated from economy 81

ideal: of Bildung 8, 46, 48, 45; British Idealism 85; self 2, 5, 32; humanist 30–1, 35, 43; humanity 2–3, 34; idealism of dialogue xxiv, 4, 6, 8, 79, 86; of liberalism in capitalism 81; meritocratic 45; modernity and organisational 63; organisational 11–12, 53; in public institution xxvii, 51, 53; in reforming Dr. S. van Mesdag Clinic 54–9; state of justice 7; technology creates xxvi, 32, 37–8; of universality xxii–iii

identity: corroded by formal power 59; denied singularity xvii; mediated by 'police order' xviii; mediated by technics 33; prerequisite for claiming right xii–xiii; and subjectification xiv–xv
Ilomäki, L. 35
imagination: of dialogue 4; of hominids, of world 3; and technics xxv–vi, 32–5; and technology in education 36–8; used in humanising prison 55
individualisation and technology 35–7
individuation; culture as transindividuation 33, 38; as process of becoming related to technology 30–8
information: ad agencies use of 69; authenticity lost through bureaucratisation of flows of 70; and biopolitical control 73; ICT xxvi, 30; ownership of 72–3; reducing complexity by organising flow of xxviii, 72, 76, 78
innovation xxi: education provides no ground for 44; national health care as 75; needs complexity 78; profit used for 85; rationalisation leaving no space for 53, 55; by rich corporation xviii; starts from interpersonal relationships 26; from vital perspective 23
institution: academic 22; as actor/object of humanisation 1–3, 6–9; (employees) alienation in public 52–3, 58; derived rights of 1; dialogue realised in 79; forensic psychiatric xxiii; and humiliation 56–7; medicine as 72; power of vertical 54, 57; public xxvi–vii; role of in health care 75; and subjectification xiv; as theatre 56
instrumental: accountability versus responsibility 45; AIDS as instrument for ordering sexuality 72; approach as *cinematographic tendency* 24; instruments in formation of subject 78; and impersonal expert logic 20–23; knowledge as instrument 73; learning 43, 45; measurement for security 42; rationality 6, 77; technology as 30–1; use of human interaction 22
interaction: 3; ad industry requires social/personal 69; in consultancy 22–6; of customer with brand 65–6; dehumanising client and employee by rationalised 52; education 36–7; of health organisation with society 74; interactionist account of ICT 39n10; mediated by language 71, 76–8; online 67–8, 70; replaced by information flows 72
intrinsic: connections of subsystems of society 8; dynamic between essential human properties 4; motivation 43, 46, 48–9; value, dignity 5
intuition 14–6; action driven by xxi; of consultants 24–7; motivating xxiii–v

Jacobs, G. 2,
Jansen, H. 30, 37
Jansen, T. 52, 53
Joinville, Brasil 74–76

Jonas, H. 3, 4, 6
Jones, L. 47
justice xxii, xxiv: identity and xiii–xiv; and speech xv, 78; to all entities of right 2, 9; dialogue and 4, 6, 82; and sense making 7, 52; as subsystem of society 8; to problems 21, 24; to complexity of education 36, 47; Department of 54; institutions of 56–8

Kant, I. 6
Kaufer, K. 51
Kempe, G (officer, WW2) 51
Kivelä, A. 41
King, Martin Luther 11
Kiviat, B. xviii
knowledge xxii: advertising based on 65; creation xxv, 20–4; *docta ignorantia* 13–14; expert xxv, 20, 25, 27; implicit/explicit 15–18; intuition and xxiv, 15–16; participation in 5, 7, 8, 9, 9; and power xxv; reflection versus professional 52; as result of thinking 13; and sense 14, 17–18, 25–6; and technics/culture 33; and uncertainty 42; values versus objective 46
Kohn, A. 30, 38
Kolind, L. 52
Kundera, M. 42, 47
Kunneman, H. 22, 37
Kurzweil, R. 31

Labour: absenteeism 54, 55; alienation from 53; as alternative punishment 51; care of self through 7, 82; for community of soul 86; *cooperative* system of 8, 79–80, 83; investment in 85; market xxiii, 42
Langer, S. 15, 16
language 50, 53, 85: as characteristic of human 3–4 (*see also* xv); and complexity xxviii; constitution of human through 77; game 74; interaction mediated by 71, 76, 78; and intuition and sense 14–15, 18; management as organisations' 11; and politics xvi–xvii; programming 35–6; and reality 11–18; and rest 16; and weak thinking 16–17; *see also* speech
Lapidus, R. xvi–xvii
law 46: bureaucratic legislation protecting inmates 51; capitalism represented by 81 (also xviii); community constituted by xii, xiv (*also* xvi); enforcement and Black Lives Matter xii; and good Inhuman xvii; about health care 75–6; first mention of humanisation in Dutch concerns criminal 50; moral 82; should represent economy for common good 84–5; and scientific management 21; state of 7, 8; quality comprises legitimacy 77
legitimation: of anthropological assumptions 4; of control in education 46; of feeling humiliated 56; legitimate self 2; of power/political goals by humanisation 57

94 *Index*

Lemmens, P. 31
lean 21, 22, 24
learning: anxiety limits xviii; skills xxv, 31–4; from problematisation xxv, 20–27; time for 24–25, 37, 46; and uncertainty xxvi, 41–9; Enlightenment as 6; learned ignorance 14; and meritocracy 45–6
Leroi-Gourhan, A. 3
Levinas, I. 47
Levinson, N. 48
Linstead, S. xxi; capacity for negativity xv; inhuman as excess xvii; organisation as engagement xi on 'reply', on *interplex* process 23
liquidity: of advertising originates in liquid modernity 63–4; iterative process of liquefying/solidifying 63; *liquid modernity* xxvii, 61; managing 69; as opportunity for humanising 70; and panopticon/synopticon 64–5; and virtual relationships 66
Lissenberg, E. 51
logic: dia logos 47; (problem solving by) expert 20–23; of ICT 35–6; *logics* of progress 7; logos and speech xvi–xv–xvi; logic/logos of technics and skill 31–2; Power Point 18
love: equality and 81; for figures 12; in humanism 34; knowledge, power and 8
Luhmann, N. xxviii; on reduction of complexity 72–3, 76
Lyotard, J. F. on language xv, xvi, xvii

machine: liberal capitalist state as 82; human interaction as cogs in 22; machine-like bureaucracy as 'inhuman' xvii; management between laissez-faire and 50; verticalisation and 53
managers: as actor in theatre 56; attention to situatedness in multiple humanising processes 7, 8; authors as xxiii; balancing control and uncertainty 41, 44, 46–8; balancing freedom and discipline 50; engaging with all stakeholders 55; ICT speaks to xxvi; ideal of agreement 12; ideal of transparency and efficiency 36, 42; making sense xxii; making employees anonymous 53; managerial expert knowledge 20; online relation to employees 67–8; of public hospital São Paolo; of psychiatric clinic 54; responsibility becomes accountability 45; role in *Panopticon/Synopticon* 64–6; self reflection 57–9
management 20: advice (critique) 17; airport literature xxv, 27n3; and ambiguity 12–13; Bildung and 41; comes after care 18; distance from everyday xxvi; and education, imagination, ICT 35–8; ethical choices of 72; of HIV/AIDS epidemic 71, 76; horizontal/vertical xxvii, 52, 57, 77; involved with stakeholders 55; as language of organisation 11–12; and liquid modernity 63, 69; models 25; (*see also knowledge (expert)*); new public xxvi, 45; as opposed to conversation 17; restricted by holding companies 62, 64; scientific 21–22; and targets 36–7, 46; theory needs philosophy 23; values of dialogue guiding 82–3
Margalit, A. xxvii, 56
Martin, G. 30
market: xviii, xxiii, xxvii; as abstraction 11–12, 16, 81; agora 86; clients want divers 64; and common good xxviii; liquefied 63; *moralisation of* 80, 82; students and labour 42; technology transforming 65
marketing *see advertising*
Marx, K. xvii, 80, 85
Matthiesen, T. 64
meaning xxi, xxiii, 5, 6, 35; give meaning to work xxii; of hidden curriculum 44; humanising as implicit ideal driving search for 18; individual exploring 7; intuition and xxiv; language and xvi, xxv, 13–16; organisations deny diversity of 12; ethos and 17; meaningful life in public organisation 52–3; meaningful character of an institution 58; original meaning of liberty 81; problematisation as search for 21; of punishment 51; sensibility and 18; technology and 30, 33, 36–7; and uncertainty 42; *see also sense*
means to ends category *see intstrumental*.
measurement: by capitalist organisation xii; critical discourse in education about 30; and expert logic 21–22; of happiness 83; learning outcomes not captured by 46; of meritocratic 45; and positivism 47; progress 7; and scientific management 21–2; short term xviii; standardisation by 37, 42; of time 22; viral load 73; of worth of ad agency 62
medicine: bureaucracy and human dimension of health care 72–4; technics is xxv, 34; medical care in prison 51; medical intertwined with social, political economic and other problems xxvii, 71; monopoly of medical fraternity 76; pharmacology 31, 34; and power 72–3
meritocracy xxvi, 36, 41; education in 45; and neglect of existential uncertainty 46–7
Merleau-Ponty, M. 4
Mission statements 11–13
modernity: economy and values of 80, 82, 86; liquid modernity 61–70;
moral: authority xii, xiv; community 5, 7; *Consciousness and Communicative Action* 71; development 6, 8, 9; domain connected to economy 86; ideological reasons for reduction not 72; insight defining the human 3; interest of AIDS victims 73; intuition 16, 21; law 82; philosophy xv; problems of organisation 20, 22; problem 20, 22, 42; reference point in theory 56; reflection 83; sensibility 18, 21; uncertainty xiv, 47; values 4

morality: of city counsel 75; communication processes question group and society's 71–72; community by shared ethos, sense and 17; 'swallowed' by targets 46
Morin, E. 4
Mul, J. de 30
Mullarkey, J. xi

nation: xi, 36; economy of 80
nature xvii, xvii, 21, 23, 52, 54, 61, 72; dignity of 5; human xiv, xxv, 4, 5, 6, 30, 32; and humanity as family 8; normative constitution of 5, 9n3; respectful use of 2; sensibility towards 6
Negri, A. xvii
Nietzsche, F. 15, 16
Nohria, N. 22
Norman, P. xi
Nussbaum, M. xxii, 34, 46, 52

Obama, B. xiii
ontology: Hegel 77; ontological foundation of abilities 4; *ontological security* 41; relational xiv
Orwell, G. xi
Ossewaarde R. 52
Ostrom, E. 85

Paech, H. 85
Panamerican Health Organisation, 77
panopticon, synopticon: xxvii, 64–66, 69, 70
participation: in dialogue xxviii, 5, 7, 17, 59; in knowledge 7; online 66; political 7, 8, 84, 85, 45; of scientist 71; in society 7, of stakeholders 72, 75, 84
Pedersen, M. 23
Philip the Second 51
philosophy: 1, 2, 52; Bergson 15, 24; Deleuzian 23; German 8; Greek 80, 82; of humanism 50; humanist xxi; of language 71, 74; and management theory 23; Marx 80; moral xv; post-modern xxi; practical 80
Piketty, T. 85
Plato 80, 85; platonic 84
policy 16, 57; adversity to sense/meaning 17; health 74–6; human-based xxvii, 69; meritocracy 36; for online representation 70; open-door 57; of organisation xxvii, 11, 12; of student 46; and practice 12; top-down 45–6
politics xi, xv, xviii, xxvii, 51, 68, 74, 75; identity xii; bio xiii, 72–3; economic as political science 47; as esthetic xv–xviii; humanisation legitimating 57; of open society 5, 7, 8; sensibility 16, 18; and speech xv, xvi, 18
Popper, K. 5
potential: xxv, 35; consumer 65; creativity 44; human xi, xxi, xxii, 2, 3, 32, 34–36; humanising xxvii, 70; learning 41, 48; for relations 53; revolutionary xvii

power: xvii, 51, 52, 55, 57, 58; and abstract thinking 3; control mechanism 54, 57; and democratic participation 7, 8; dialogical 4, 5; and economic participation 8; formal 59; of negation 15 with politics xvi; purchasing xviii; structures xxvii, 52, 57; relations xvii, 50; society 45; of speech xv; use of xxvi, 72
Prahalad, C. K. xviii
predictable: control 63, 64; learning 42; learning not 47; and organisations 73; predictability 53, 63; routines 41
private: companies 7, 82; Facebook page 67; lives 30, 66, 67; network 70; plans 75; property 80, 81
problems: xxv, xxviii, 24, 26, 27, 52; health 71, 74; to humanisation 50, 52; of management 77; medical xxvii; moral, existential 20, 22; organisational 24, 25, 72; practical 47; social xviii, 23, 25; *wicked* xxv, 20, 22
problematisation xxv, 20–27
process xiv, xxvii, 35, 53, 58, 59, 77, 82, 84; of becoming 32, 33, 37; Bildung 41, 48, 83; of civilisation, enlightenment 6; communication xxi, 56, 71; creative 41; cultural 3, 5; of democratisation 7, 8; of development 36, 38; historical xxiv, 1, 50; *human value* by dialogical 21, 30, 31, 47; of humanisation xxiii, xxv, 34, 37, 50, 51, 54, 56, 61, 65, 79, 83; humanisation as dialogical, reflective 1–3; of intellectual sympathy 24; of interaction 37; of learning xxvi, 42–45, 77; liquefying 63; of mission statement 13; of modernity 63; organisational development xxi, xxii, 57, 72; political xii; problematisation as vital 21–23, 26; of reducing complexity 72, 73; of self-determination xviii; social 74, 77; rationalisation 63; technical 38
professional 26, 36, 45, 55; action 52, 53; autonomy 49; chances 70; commitment 46; corporations 74; dilemma's xxv; field of expertise 37; in health 71, 73–77; judgement 45; knowledge 24, 46, 52; life xxvii, 61, 67; pride 53; in relation to personal 65, 67–69; relationships xxiv, 67; teachers 47; themes 68; transition 74; treatment 55
profit xviii, 21, 52, 53, 55, 81, 83, 84; financial 85; margin 62; organisations 30
progress: in cultural history 3, 7; duration (time) as 24, 59; human civilisation 63; *interplex* 23
Prometheus 32
Proulx, M. 66
public xviii, xxv, xxvi, 55, 56, 68, 72–74; accountability xviii; good xviii, 53; health service 71, 74, 75, 77; humiliation 51; institutions xxvi, 57; life 66; new management xxvi, 45; network 70; opinion 70; organisations 30, 52, 53, 55, 58, 59; relationships 66, 68, 69; social order 51, 52; stock exchange 62

quality xxv, 55; air xiii; of care 76, 77; human xiv, 32; of education 37, 42; of ICT 37; of managers 56; of organisation 52; product and services 55; of work 35, 43, 62, 64

Radkau, J. 85
Ranciere, J. xii, xiv, xvii; on evil xiii, xviii; on politics xvi; on subjectivity xv
rationality: creation and pre-linguistic 17; instrumental 6; and other characteristic of humanity 3, 4; of scientific management 21
rationalisation: bureaucratisation and 53, 73; of feelings 3–4; and humiliation 50; medical 73, 76; non-instrumental, enlightenment and civilisation 6
reality: abstraction, imagination and 3; of everyday life 24; language and 11–18, 71, 80; of network society 30; use of theory for structuring 56
reflective: capacities and enlightenment 6; control of individual 1; cultural processes 2; turn through problematisation 26–27; unreflective machines 53
reflection xxiii, 44, 52, 54, 82, 83; critical 42, 43; educational 53; as human characteristic 4; philosophical xxiv, 80; on power relations 50, 51; as presentative ideal inviting 16; on problem 24; stops after articulation 13, 18; moral 47; self 52, 57
recognition xxvi, 4, 16, 36, 37, 46, 52; of equality 82; of subjectivity xvi
Renaissance xxiii, 34, 51
responsibility xxi, xxviii, 45, 52, 55, 66; in advertising 69; corporate social 83; for development, rationalisation leading to 6; in education 41–44, 47, 49; innate moral imperatives of 9, 79, 80; normative, transcendental ideal 4; self 82; social xviii, xxiv, 84
Richardson, J. R. xii
rights xii–xv, xviii, 52, 81–83, 85; and capabilities 3, 34; in economy of competition 81–2, 85; in human essence 4–5; civil xi; human and non-human 1–2, 4–9, 83; human rights xi–xv, 34, 73–75; over planet xi; political ascription of identity, (in)humanity and (human) xi–xviii; private property as 81; rightholders as *terminus ad quem* of humanisation 1–2, 6, 7; state based on 8; of subjects of public organisation 52
Rittel, H. 22
romantic: German xxvi; romanticism xxiv, 6, 30
Rousseau, J.-J. 6
Ruller, S. van 51

São Paulo 72, 77
Sarmiento, D. 5
Saussure, F. de 15
Scharmer, C. O. 51, 53

Schellhammer, B. 48
science 2, 8, 14, 47, 80; of economy xxviii, 80, 81; educational 41, 45; exact 46; information 71; and management 21–22; political 47; social xxiii, 73, 74; technique and 77
scientific: conflicts 72; ideas opposed to intuition 27; insights 8; knowledge detached from life 24; management 21; models 72, 73
self-direction 51, 59; human 50; as humanisation at micro-level 1; in organisations 51, 55, 58; professional action and 52, 53; and restriction of autonomy 56
Sennet, R. 30
sensibility xxii, 59; consultancy stimulating organisations 25–27; creating a xxv; *human value* born of 21; humanising as 18; presentative thinking as 16; towards nature 6
sense xi, xiv, xxi, 31, 42, 45, 48, 53, 85; of accomplishment 49; and articulation 11–18; of control 36; ethical 37; humanisation ideal based in 18; humanisation rendered senseless 82; making xxii, 7, 47, 52, 56, 67, 72, 73, 81; problematisation as humanising search for 20–27; of responsibility xviii, 6; of safety 41
service: 22, 55, 61; advertising 62, 64, 65; good xxvii; financial 66; health 71, 74; providers 75; public xxv, xxvii, 53
Siebeneichler, F.B. 71
Sievers, B. xii
Siljander, P. 41
Silva, J. da 31
Simondon, G. 35
Simons, H. 12
situatedness i; hermeneutical xxiii; inhuman 56; meaningful 14; as normative perspective 7
skill: xxv, xxvi, 4, 20, 23, 36, 37, 46, 62; to change 34; imagination and 38; learning as 32; relation to ethics 33; shared 33; technics as 31, 32; technology 65, 66; in therapy 35
Smith, A. 86
Smith, T. xi
society xxvii, 1, 31–35, 38, 52, 56, 57, 62, 75, 81–85; alienation and closed 7; capitalist 79, 80; contemporary 37, 62, 67; Dutch xxiii; expressing dialogical reason 8; five subsystems of 7–8; Greek 33; humanisation of xxiv, 6, 80; incorporated into xvi; at large xxi; liquefication of 64; local 74; xxvii, 61, 72, 74, 75; meritocratic xxiv, 42, 45, 46; modern 80; network 31; open and closed 5, 7; process focussed 63; structure of authority versus participation 7, 8; transformed by historical processes 2; the Viewer 63; Western xxviii, 46
Socrates 26, 27, 47
Sørensen, B. M. 23

speech: ban on 51; as cultural development 3, 76, 78; as directive 72, 73; emphatic 57; as ethical action 71; and ethos 17; power of xv, 76; proliferation of 73; speechless intuition 15; stuttering 17, 18
stakeholders: in dialogue with xxii, xxiv, 25, 27, 77, 84; of organisations 2, 26, 36
standardisation: part of bureaucratisation 53; part of education 37, 42; by scientific management 21
Stelter, B. 68
Stehr, N. 80
Stiegler, B. xxv, 31–39; on care 33, 35; and culture 33; and logos 32, 35; pharmacology 34; philosophical anthropology 31; transindividuation 38
strategy: CRS 84; of humanisation process 54; human rights 75; and language reality 11–12, 16; medical 73, 76; at meso-level 2; political 72; of survival 83
structure: authoritarian 8; of dialogue xxiv, 4, 6; of economy 84, 85; education 42, 44, 48; essential xxv; financial 86; as goal 44, 46; of hermeneutic circle 2; hierarchical 52, 63; of immaturity 6; of information flows 72, 78; of mind and consciousness 5; organisational xxii, xxvi; power xxvii, 52, 57, 58; processes and xxiii; social 85; of societies xxiv, 8, 9; and solidification 63, 64, 70; as theatre in Goffman 56; transcendental 4
subject: as different from object 14; encounter between student and 47; egoistic 80; individual 1; need to communicate 71; philosophical research 1; as problem for moral philosophy xv; phonocentric xv; to 'seinsvergessenheid' 42; sharing a common world xvi; as speaking xv; subjective happiness 5, 7; as sustainability 26; transcendental xv; unknowable 14
subjection: as adaption 33; assertion of singularity xiv; categorisations as xiv; creative xv; to demands 33; making yourself appear as xiv; to power 57; to rules and procedures 58; to strict procedures 43; to technologies xxv
Summers, L. xiii
Sutinen, A 42
Swaaningen, R. van 51
Swierstra, T. 36, 38
Styhre, A. 22
symbolic act xi; industry of the xvii; location 36; violence xvi
system: of accountability 48; authoritarian 7; belief xxvii, 62; to blame 45; of care 7, 8; of competition 82; of control xxvi, 35, 37, 58; of corporation 80, 86; to democracy 84; disappear in 35; distrust 82; of eco 1, 2; economic xxviii, 78–80, 86; ethical xii; of general participation 2, 79; Greek 80;

health 75; to ideals 63, 79; of justice 57; meritocracy as social 45; National Health 76; operating 65; organisational 52, 53; organisations as 23; versus people 53; of political participation 8, 57, 82; prison 50, 56; production 53; punishment 51; rules and 53; as part of solutions 20; standardised 52; subsystems of society 7–9; systematic approach of consultancy 22; systematic management 21; systematic theory xxii; technological 31, 35; theory (Luhmann) 72, 85; world of 57, 71, 78

tacit: and implicit knowledge 17, 18; pressure 67
Taylor, Ch. 1, 2
Taylor, F. 21
technical: bureaucratic structure 46; focus of management 20–21; interest in 76; knowledge's use 22; maieutics 31; organisations as flow not 23; part of organology 35; philosophical anthropology and 31; system 23
technics: and autonomy 35; and care 34; logos as discourse on 32; as skill 31; and time 31; and tools 3
technology: in add agencies 64, 65; affordance by 63; and humanisation 30–40; liquid modernity and 64; medical 74; revolution 65; struggles with 61
Thatcher, M. 81
thinking: driven by sense, care, and weak- 15–18; essential to humanity 3, 4; intuition as 15; starts from not-knowing 13–14
Tienda, M. 45
time: air 51; to become skilled xxv; compress 63; and culture 33; developing into autonomous being takes 37; ethics based in 33; fixed 41; management related 13; measuring 22; the need to take and waste 24, 27; technics and 31; real 64; slots 45; technocratic 46; technology creating 34
transformation: ecological 7; in communication 62; of global economy 84; of interpersonal relationships 66; meaning 15, 16; of society 80; by technology 65; from welfarism to new managerialism 46
transparency: and efficiency xxvi, 36, 37; as norm 42, 45
trust: distrust in police apparatus xviii; in language 15; in definitions 15; basic 41; systems of distrust 82
Tonkens, E. 36, 38
tool: creating shared meaning 33; early use of 3; humanisation as 57; human and tool invent each other 31; personal experience as 26; of social control 73
Toppin, G. 20
truth: claims of science challenged by organisational living reality 24;

against superstition 63; system of knowledge and 8; thinking in relation 17; truthfulness in communication 6; universal i; will to 7

United Nations 77
uncertainty: advertising industry and 61, 62, 69; of being human xxii; consequence of liquidity 69; and education 42–49; wisdom of xxvi, 42
universal: Declaration of Human Right 5; dialogical values xxii; ethics xiv,1; moral community 5; solidarity 85; truths i; *see also knowledge (expert)*

Varoufakis, Y. 86
value: basic xii; core 2; corporations' ultimate 84; dialogical xxii, 38, 80, 82; of dialogue 20–21; ethical 56, 81; human 30, 38, 58, 82; humanist 81; in ICT 35; of implicit knowledge 18; intrinsic 5; of modernity 80–82; moral xii, 4; of responsibility 47; shareholder xvii, 52; spiritual 52; of unclearness 12
Vattimo, G. 17
Verbeek, P.-P. 30
Verbrugge, A. 53
Vinge, V. 31
violence: decrease of humiliation, torture and death 50; disappearance of 8, 9; economic system build on xxviii, 80; non- xxvi; and punishment 51; renouncement of 84; symbolic xvi

Wal, K. van der 81
Webber, M. 22
Weber, M. 86
Weick, C. xxii
Welzer, H. 84
William of Orange 51
Wittgenstein, L. 47
work: advisory 30; digital 66; good 30, 37; medical 74; organisational processes as repetition of 23; places 57, 62–66; quality 62; satisfaction 58; skilled 37; virtuous xviii
world: agency 66; alienation by technology 31; articulation of desirable 3; Bank xiii; changing 42, 63; common xvi; control of 13, 18; dialogical relation to 4; digital 64; economy as control of 8; engage with 32; future 32; humane 1, 2; and imagination/thought 3; from known to new 23; making sense of 7; natural 6; private 67; ready-made versus general understanding of 24; real different from discursive, known 14, 16–17; righteous 41; of social media 68; system- and life 57, 75